Never Going Back

The Gordon Ferguson Story

Lessons from a Life
of Courage, Strength and Love

I couldn't put it down. It is very well-written and organized. Gord's voice is strong and powerful and I can hear him saying all those words as if he had read it aloud to me. I loved all the wonderful photos, too. As a colleague of his, I learned a lot more about him and his remarkable life. What a recorded legacy he has left for everyone.
Nancy McNamara, Board Member, BDACI

A tireless disability advocate can now add author to a long list of accomplishments.
Book review by *Ron Laroche*, Community Living Ontario in *Update Friday*, May 27, 2016

Decades after he was admitted to Rideau [Regional Centre], he helped close it down. Ferguson has spent his life outside of the institution as a voice for individuals with developmental disabilities. He has been an advocate in the community sharing first-hand experiences about the adversity that he has faced over his lifetime. He hopes by sharing his story he can stop his narrative from repeating.

Ali Wilson, The Recorder and Times, June 7, 2016

Never Going Back

The Gordon Ferguson Story

Lessons from a Life
of Courage, Strength and Love

Gordon Ferguson
with Harry van Bommel

Resources Supporting Family and
Community Legacies Inc.
A *Canada 150* Series Publication
Toronto 2016

Library and Archives Canada Cataloguing in Publication

Ferguson, Gordon, 1948-, author
    **Never going back : the Gordon Ferguson story :
lessons from a life of
courage, strength and love / Gordon Ferguson with Harry
van Bommel.**

Includes index.

ISBN 978-1-55307-092-4 (paperback)

        **1. Ferguson, Gordon, 1948-. 2. Ferguson, Gordon,
1948- --Childhood and
youth. 3. Developmentally disabled--Ontario--Biography.
4. Developmentally
disabled--Family relationships--Ontario. I. Van Bommel,
Harry, author
II. Title. III. Title: Gordon Ferguson story.**

HV1570.5.C3F47 2016   362.19680092   C2016-902156-4

Contact BDACI at:

2495 Parkdale Avenue

Brockville, ON   K6V 3H2

613.345.4092

bdaci@ripnet.com

This book is dedicated to my wife Donna
who makes everything I do possible.

In memory of my mother, Audrey,
who did the best she could and who loved me very much.

In memory of Beth French, my friend, neighbour and
Executive Director of the Brockville & District Association
for Community Involvement, who always believed in me.

In thanks to my many friends and my colleagues at the
Brockville and District Association for Community
Involvement who have helped me through the decades turn
my dreams into reality.

Table of Contents

Foreword

We keep each other alive with our stories.
We need to share them, as much as we need
to share food. We also require for our health
the presence of good companions.
Barry López in **Arctic Dreams**

Gordon Ferguson has lived a history that everyone who cares about building just and inclusive communities must understand. He has composed a good life by navigating the issues that have defined and redefined life for people with intellectual disabilities since his birth in 1948.

Gord has overcome some of the worst that society can inflict of those who are devalued because of their differences. Excluded from school at age 8, separated from his family and exiled to a 2,000-person institution at age ten, he experienced 16 years of indignity, neglect of the professional duty to educate, deprivation of choice, hard work for tiny wages, and abuses, some, he tells us, still too traumatic to share with readers.

Since his emancipation from the institution, he has made the best of the opportunities opened by a growing alignment of necessary support with the intentional creation and defence of valued social roles. After escaping the institution he has been a trail-blazer in marriage, home ownership, work, governance of civic associations and advocacy.

Here is a life of full citizenship. Husband, home owner, worker, driver, collector: roles that seem so ordinary as to be unremarkable until these chapters account how difficult they have been to establish and how vulnerable they remain. And there are civic roles, responsibilities to the whole community, that Gord has capably discharged for decades. Board member, committee member, People First organizer – long term roles that have satisfied both his desire to make things better for everyone at risk of exclusion and his lifelong interest in learning.

He has developed and advocates for thoughtful positions on critical issues. In the pages that follow, he shares insight into the right course to take on the abolition of institutions and vigilance against the threat of their re-emergence in the form of nursing homes, on what a real home is and why home ownership matters, on supported decision making, on individualized funding, on the qualities of good supporters, on involuntary sterilization, on selective abortion, on euthanasia.

Valued roles are available to Gord not only because he is a gifted man who is deeply committed to live as a full citizen, but also because he lives in a community that has worked intentionally, persistently and creatively for more than 25 years to do the slow and difficult work of building a community that welcomes, respects and supports the contributions of people with intellectual disabilities.

Too many other communities have yet to undertake this work with the commitment it demands and government policy is sluggish in its attempts to catch up to Gord, his wife Donna and their friends. May these stories enliven the journeys of those in less fortunate communities and in Government offices.

Gord makes no secret that he has been hurt and remains vulnerable, especially to people who assume that they know better than he does, but he does not identify himself as a victim, neither has he lived that way. He writes this book as a contribution to his own healing and to the healing of our wounded society. The wisdom born of his gifts of reflection, appreciated by those who have shared board tables with him, make this book an expression of his role as a teacher.

These are the stories of a man who finds ways to engage his energy and strengths in service to others. It does not give too much away to preview his key to a good life: a web of diverse, long term relationships embodied in a variety of contributing social roles.   *John O'Brien*

Introduction

Be bold enough to use your voice,
Brave enough to listen to your heart,
And strong enough to live the life
You've always imagined.
  Anonymous

I am a lucky man. I have been bold enough, brave enough
and strong enough through the best parts of my life because
I am surrounded by people who love me and who like me for
the man I am.

I am a lucky man to have escaped the Rideau Regional
Centre in Smiths Falls, Ontario – I wish it had been sooner
or that I had never gone there at all. There were a few good
people there including many friends, but on the whole, I
would rather have lived in my own home and in my own
community.

I am a lucky man because I met Donna, my wife. We complement each other. When I am shy, she is dragging me onto the dance floor. When she is worried about something, I am there to cuddle her and help her.

I am a lucky man because people think my story is worth publishing.

I am lucky that I have readers like you interested in not only my stories but also in the lessons I have learned. Some people have called me wise. I don't know about that. I think if you live long enough, you learn a lot and if other people are interested in what you've learned, then your life has meaning.

I would love to live forever because there is still more that I want to do. But that will not happen for any of us. So I hope that my experiences will be interesting and helpful to you. Even though we may never meet, I feel honoured to share my stories of courage, strength and love with you.

Acknowledgements

The best part of writing a book is that you have a place to formally thank all the people who are important in your life. So thank you to all of my family, friends and colleagues who have enriched my life and given me experiences that have led to this book.

In particular, I want to thank:

My wife, Donna, for sharing the best parts of my life with me and for giving me so many memories worth keeping – some of them in this book.

Denise Wright who has really made this book possible. She listened to all my stories, scanned photographs, passed on the information to Harry van Bommel who put the book all together, and she did it with genuine love in her heart. I am so grateful.

Margo Leclair for designing the cover of my book.

Peg Jenner, Jane Barken and Denise Wright who provided the Student/Book Club Questions at the end of the book.

My editing team: Kathy Senneker, Peter Leclair, Dianne Hickling, Nancy McNamara, Doug Mather, Harry Pott, Melissa Latimer, Caroline Brown, and Denise Wright.

The trustees of my mother's Will who listened to me, believed in me and trusted me to be able to live the life that I wanted in my own home with my wife. I do not hold any hard feelings. I know that you acted out of concern and love.

My cousins Ron and Shirley whose friendship was the best part of my childhood.

The five families who loaned me money so that Donna and I could keep our house. You have no idea how much Donna and I appreciate what you have done for us. You saved us. Thank you.

Doug Cartan who has been my friend, my advisor and my protector. If it wasn't for you my life would be very different today. You always encouraged me and gave me confidence to try things. I thank you very much for standing by me through the hard times, especially when my home was threatened. I think of you like my new big "S" TV…. A smart one.

My circle, who have been there for Donna and me. Our times together are always filled with lots of laughter, talk and music. We are a fantastic team. I feel like I am surrounded by people who care and want the best for us.

My support staff, who are what good support should be. With you, Donna and my needs are looked after; we go out, we do our work and we have fun doing it. You make us feel safe, you share our interests, you listen to us, you make us laugh and you still get the job done.

The Leeds & Grenville Service Providers, Developmental Services Ontario and the Ministry of Community & Social Services for believing in Donna and me, and somehow always being able to find enough support funding so that we could live at home.

Lastly, to the Board of Directors of the Brockville and District Association for Community Involvement for their encouragement and their financial support to make this book possible. Having sat on the board for many years, I feel especially proud to have them recognize my work and my life. May it help others in the future.

Chapter 1   Lessons Learned

Usually one ends a book with a chapter about the lessons
they have learned. I want to start with my lessons because
they took me a lifetime to learn and I want to share them
first. We often have to make our own mistakes and achieve
our own successes, but sometimes we can learn from others
to avoid some of their heartache. I think these lessons may
help others.

Planning with the Person Involved

Most of the heartaches in my life have come about because other people thought they knew what was best for me. They thought their opinion was right and they didn't listen to what I wanted.

They were wrong.

The person at the centre of decisions needs to be the boss of their own plan. Things don't always happen in the way you think it will happen. When making a plan you need to include lots of people but the person at the centre must be in control as much as possible. Everyone has to listen carefully.

To have the best plan, make rules at the beginning. Have everybody agree who is the boss, what the goals of the plan are and what we all want to see happen, and not happen.

I was upset when people would not listen to me. Sometimes people disagreed with me and sometimes I disagreed with them. When that happens, everyone needs to be more open and listen even better.

I hope that other people can avoid being bullied into making decisions. People often mean well, but bullying is never a fair way to reach a decision. My mom and I loved each other very much, but we disagreed on some things. We should have worked out our differences in a different way, but it was so hard. Often people didn't like my answer, so they ignored what I said. I used to get into fights with my mother and others when they would not listen. Then I stopped talking. It was just easier to stay quiet and worry inside. That was wrong. It hurt all of us terribly and it was not necessary.

A Good Life is Worth Fighting For

The good things in life are worth fighting for. It takes a lot of planning and work to make something happen.

Sometimes you win and sometimes you lose. Each win and loss teaches you something you can use in your next fight for a good life.

If it is important enough to you, don't give up. There were lots of times that I was feeling angry, hopeless, ready to give up and run away. My friends were there to help me think of different ways to act and to give me hope.

Sometimes I wish I did not have to fight for everything though. Why can't some things be easy to accomplish like opening a bank account, buying a home, getting a job? Why do so many things need to be a struggle – not just for me or for people with disabilities, but for everyone? Why can't we adapt the rules to make them work for all people? Why can't we create systems that are centred around people's needs rather than on bureaucracy?

Nursing Homes are Institutions, not Homes

My mother wanted my wife Donna and me to move into a nursing home after she died. She wanted us to give up our home. When I got out of Rideau, after 16 long years, I promised myself that I was never going back to an institution. A nursing home is an institution.

Living in my home is different than living in an institution. When I am home, it is mine. I can make it my own. I can do whatever I want to do. I am comfortable and can relax here. It's the place I want to be. I have my stuff here. I feel happy seeing Donna so happy. I can joke around with her here. After my mom died, I moved things around in the house. I changed to a bigger bed. Donna switched rooms. We changed the living room furniture and how it was laid out.

We could do all of that because it was our home. We cannot be kicked out and forced to move. Even better we have a great investment in our home that keeps growing in value.

Money Gives You Choices and Control

Many people do not think enough about their money. If
they want something they buy it. They don't think about their
bills. They hope everything will turn out okay. Well, it won't.
If you spend all your money, you won't have any left.

Buying our own home and getting a mortgage was a big
problem. I did not want Donna to sign a bank loan. I did not
want them to question whether or not she understood what
she was signing. Because we are married, this is her home
and no one would loan me the money without Donna's
signature, even though the house is only in my name.

Fortunately our friends came to the rescue, and loaned us
enough money to pay off our bills. These friends understood
how important it was for us to keep our home. They are
amazing.

Legal Issues are Complicated

A lawyer can help you fight for what you want. My mother's
Last Will and Testament made the trustees try to force us to
go to a nursing home. As I've already written, we did not
want to live in an institution. Even my mother didn't want to
live in a nursing home herself but she thought Donna and I
would be safer there. I don't think we would be safer cut off
from all of our friends. We are safer in our own home.

Sometimes, you need to hire a lawyer. Lawyers are very
expensive and without my friends I wouldn't have been able
to afford one.

I wish my mother had not tried to use her Will as a way to
get Donna and me to live in a nursing home. People should
not use their Will to do things for them after they have died.
Mom could not convince us to move into a nursing home
when she was alive, so she tried to force us to do it after she
died. She meant well but she was wrong. It caused all sorts of

problems, heartaches and anxiety that were not necessary for anyone.

Everyone needs to plan for the future. When you plan, use a good lawyer to make sure the legal parts of the plan (e.g., buying a house) are done right. Do not assume that everyone will do what you want them to do, so have your own lawyer working for you.

If you have a developmental disability, there is always the legal question about whether you understand enough to make your own decisions. Having your friends and family around you can help you be safe. Start early in the person's life and get lots of friends around the person. Make sure that they get to know the person and what they like and want. Help the person make decisions all through their life with their friends' advice. Sometimes the law makes it difficult for people to make decisions.

Note: If you have a guardian then it no longer matters what you want. It is no longer your choice. Someone else makes all the decisions for you. By having a circle or a group of people who know you well, takes the pressure off of one person. Different people can do different things, that way nobody gets tired. One person can help with one thing, and somebody else can do something else. When we talk about issues having lots of people involved it means that we can work together to make good decisions. We have to find a way to listen to people and help them make their own decisions. Instead of guardianship, we need a group of people who will help her or him make good decisions. We need a law that allows for "Supportive Decision Making."

Another legal issue is a discretionary trust for people with disabilities. Discretionary Trusts can be both good and bad. You need to have both trustees and beneficiaries. Often families pick the same people to be both. This is a really bad idea. It is what is called a "conflict of interest." People always have good intentions. They start off wanting to do well and think that everything will be easy and fine. After a while, problems happen and people get tired. Don't set up your family to fight over money. Make your favourite charity the beneficiary of the trust. That way you know that the person's needs will always be looked after first. There is no conflict of interest this way.

Valued Roles Really Do Make a Difference

Roles are important and give me a purpose. They are the reason that I get up in the morning. I have many different types of roles. I am a husband, dog owner, homeowner, cousin, neighbour, advocate, board member, collector and volunteer. Each of my roles is important. I have work to do. I matter.

Being a homeowner, for example, made me more responsible. I had to think about lots of things, like bills, and hiring someone to cut the grass. It gave me more things to think about. It's a good thing. I am now thinking about renovations, like getting a ramp. I am the boss.

I have met all of my best friends because I had roles that mattered. I have been a BDACI board member since 1991. It will be 25 years during this 60th anniversary year. The board appreciates what I have done and they have helped me in return. I like talking to them about things that matter.

When I worked I met some wonderful friends through that as well as through volunteer work. I founded the Brockville People First chapter and still have many wonderful friends through there. Pat Worth and Peter Park – both pioneers in the People First movement in Canada, mentored me. Donna's Maid of Honour was Elizabeth Sahl the President of People First Brockville. We are still close friends with her today.

In my work with *People First* we looked at issues like sterilization of women against their wills, changing the name of organizations across Canada to *Associations for Community Living*, the dangers of euthanasia for disabled people, selective abortions for babies who might be disabled, and we looked at how to close institutions. This last one is what I am most proud of. This was important because I remembered how the staff treated me and other people who were still living there.

All of these issues were very important and our voice was being listened to by people who made decisions on our behalf. My role as a leader in Brockville, meant that the members in our region had a voice – for many, it was the first time they were listened to at such a high level.

My hobbies and love of music have also brought me in contact with wonderful people who share similar interests. All of these roles mean that I can be an active participant in my community.

Living in an institution, whether Rideau Regional Centre or a nursing home, leaves you only the role of victim, patient, or resident with few rights and freedoms. There are no positive roles for people who live in these institutions. That is why I am so glad I helped to close down Rideau in March 2009.

Friends Make a Big Difference in Your Life

Last but not least, it is so important to have friends. Friendships work two ways. To have friends you must be a friend. Sometimes you give, sometimes you take. We call some of my friends 'my circle.' I am happy with them and they are happy with me. It makes me feel like I have people I can talk to if I have a problem. I can talk to all of them or any single member of the circle. I think having a big circle of friends is better than a small circle. It makes me feel like people care. It feels good to talk about things with my friends. Sometimes you need your friends more than other times.

It is important to have friends who know about things that you do not. Having friends with legal or financial or community or healthcare contacts and resources makes everything else so much easier.

There are good people out there. Don't be afraid to ask for help. My friends did something extraordinary. They helped me out with money problems. Sometimes you need more than one person helping. That also means that you have to help out when you can too.

Two things that make friendships easier are living close to them and having shared interests. The fact that I can be at your house in 10 minutes, or you can be at mine, makes it easier for us to be friends. When you live far away from people it is hard to do that.

My advocacy work, my hobbies and interests are all ways that have made friendships easier. Too often people with disabilities have one-way friendships that feel more like charity. True friendship comes when both people have gifts to offer and are encouraged to ask for help.

An example of deep friendship has been the friends who helped us keep our home. Our house was finally put in my name just before my 65th birthday. What a great birthday present. Donna and I threw a big party and invited all of our friends. Donna made really nice birdhouses for each of our friends. We made nice thank-you cards with a photo of Donna and me in front of our house. We hope they don't forget how much we appreciated what they did for us.

The rest of the book goes into more details about these lessons. I just wanted to make sure that you read about the most important lessons I've learned in my long life. There are many others, of course, but these are the main ones that come to my mind. You may even want to spend a few minutes writing down some of your own most important lessons learned. I bet you and I have some of the same ones.

Chapter 2   Childhood

I was born on Friday, September 10, 1948. Nine years before, Canada joined England and France by declaring war on Germany. It is also the day that Margaret Trudeau, the mother of our Prime Minister, was born. I keep good company with my birthday.

My Aunt Jean Gibson (her husband was my mother's brother) wrote that: "Gord was an active busy child. Very curious. He has always pushed the limits and gone beyond what we expected of him. His mother, Audrey, was very proud of Gord. She was a strong woman. Strong mentally and physically. I remember Gord as a child at their cottage. Other than that I hardly ever saw Gord as a child as he was at Rideau."

[Gord in Grade 2]

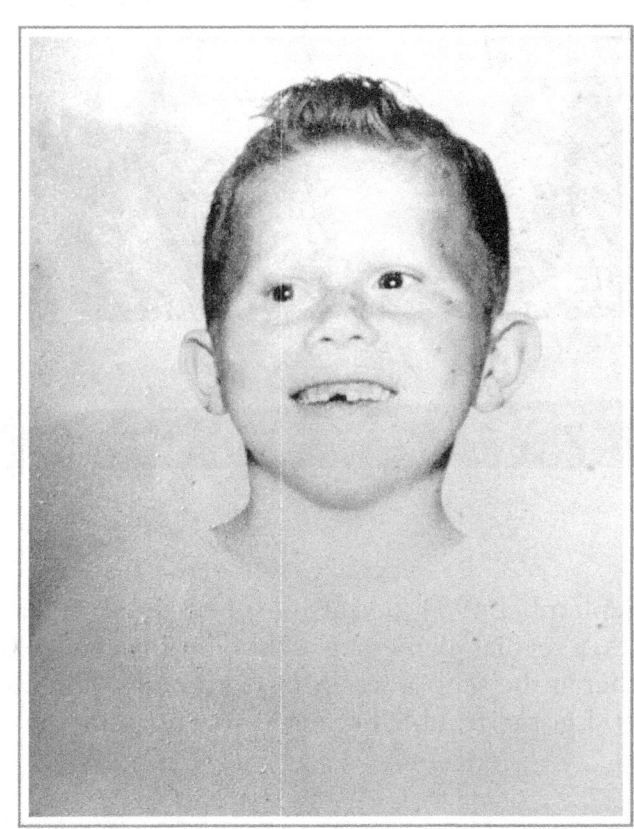

I am told that I was a busy little boy. I was always curious and getting into trouble. When I was two years old, we were visiting one of my uncle's farms and I found a water pump. I watched it for a while and wondered what it was. It didn't take long before

I was touching it and sticking my hand in the gears to see how it worked. It ate my hand. That day, I lost my thumb and two fingers.

What I remember best from that time, is my Grandma Gibson. I used to love going into her room while she stayed at our house. I would sneak into her room after my bedtime, talk to her for hours, watch her give herself her diabetic needles, listen to her stories and often fall asleep right next to her in her bed. There is a special bond between children and grandparents. I wish I had more time with her.

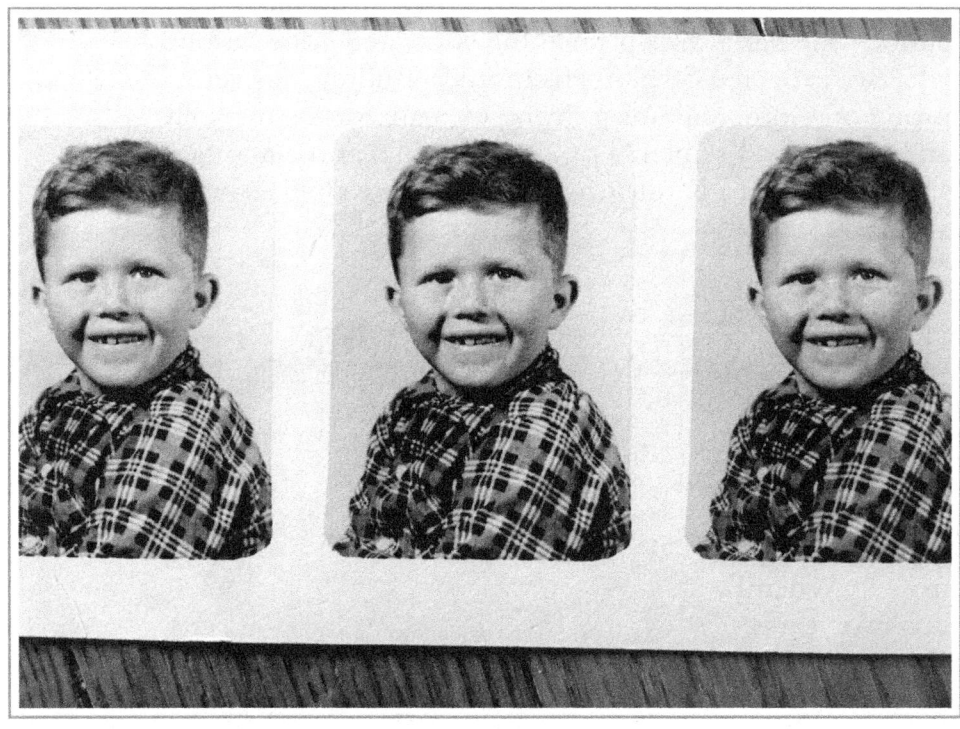

[Gord in Grade 1]

In September 1954 (6 years old) I began school at Prince of Wales, a regular elementary school in Brockville, Ontario. My teacher at the school was Mrs. Cummings. She was very strict. I got in trouble because I was bugging the other kids.

The work was hard for me and it didn't make sense, so I would rather play with my friends instead of working.

Remember in those days there were no Educational Assistants, no special help or support for kids who did not learn in the usual way. They expelled the "problem kids" from school.

They kicked me out of school in November of 1956 when I was eight years old because I wasn't doing my work and I spent too much time bugging the other kids. They said I was acting out too much. They wouldn't let me go back.

For the next year and a half, my mom home-schooled me. She wanted me to get an education. She bought books and taught me to read and do math. I was good in math. Sometimes we went to visit my aunts during this time.

My mom was always looking for a school that would take me. We could not find one. In August 1957, mom asked if I could go back to Prince of Wales and they said no. My mom was mad. She wanted me to go to school. I wanted to go to school, but they didn't care.

We then went to see Dr. Bracken, our family doctor, to see if he could help and he told us about the Ontario Hospital School in Smiths Falls.

He wrote a letter to them and recommended me. Mom and I visited the Ontario Hospital School. Dr Frank, the head doctor wrote back to my family doctor and said *"The mother reports satisfactory behaviour in the community, and I can see no reason for his not being capable of attending auxiliary classes. Many of such children profit considerably more from community placement than they do within the hospital environment and I believe that this boy will adjust very well within a specialized class placement."*

Unfortunately there was no space at the time so we had to wait.

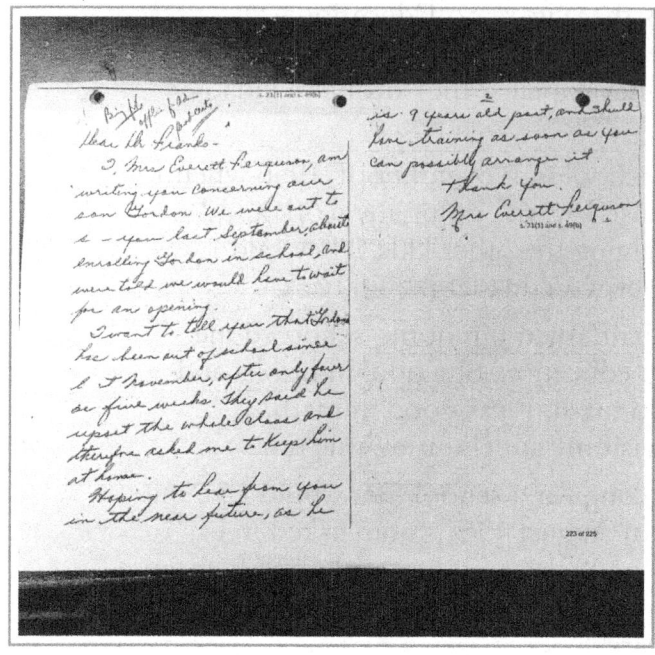

Mom grew impatient and wrote to Dr. Frank. She wrote:

Dear Dr. Frank. I, Mrs Everett Ferguson, am writing to you concerning our son Gordon. We were out to see you last September, about enrolling Gordon in school, and were told we would have to wait for an opening.

I want to tell you that Gordon has been out of school since last November, after only four or five weeks. They said he upset the whole class and therefore asked me to keep him at home.

Hoping to hear from you in the near future, as he is 9 years old past, and should have training as soon as you can possibly arrange it.

Thank you. Mrs Everett Ferguson.

Since we couldn't find another school, The Ontario Hospital School seemed to be our only hope. My mom told me it was a boarding school. We were pretty excited when they finally agreed and said that I could go. At last, I was going to get to go to school!

I moved into my new boarding school on June 23, 1958 at nearly 10 years old. Actually, when I first got there it was called the Ontario Hospital School. In 1967 they changed it to the Rideau Regional Hospital School and the year I left is when they changed the name one more time to the Rideau Regional Centre (RRC). I am going to call it by "Rideau" since that is what I call it now.

The first problem was that I wasn't allowed to go home for the first few months because they said that "I needed to get used to" the new school. The second problem was that it was June. There was no school starting until September. I don't know why I had to move in June. I don't know why I had to waste my summer in there when I wasn't going to school. But, that was just what they made me do.

I attended the school from September 1959 until March 1964 when I was nearly 16.

Aunt Jean said that she can't remember the years I was at Rideau because I had few visitors there. "I have no idea of what Gord's life was like when he lived in Smiths Falls [Rideau]. It was never spoken of."

That's a common experience for those of us who lived there. There was a shame in the community and within some families of knowing anyone who lived there. It was a distant place even for those who lived nearby. It was just 'never spoken of.'

Chapter 3   Rideau Regional Centre

Rideau Regional Centre -- Background

From June 23, 1958 until October 1974 (over 16 years!) I lived at the Rideau Regional Centre.

The Centre had over 2,000 people living there plus about the same number of staff. It was like a big town in the 60's but with much less freedom. From the Ministry of Community and Social Services website it says:

> When Ontario built its first institution for people with a developmental disability, attitudes towards people with disabilities were very different from what they are now. People were viewed as patients who needed to be treated, cared for and protected.
>
> Institutions, therefore, provided a medical model of care that focused primarily on the health of the residents.
>
> In keeping with the attitudes of the time, the Ontario Department of Health was originally responsible for Ontario's institutions for people with a developmental disability.
>
> It wasn't until 1974 with the shift from institutionalization to community living well underway that the Ministry of Community and Social Services took over responsibility for services for people with a developmental disability. [access Feb 20, 2016: *www.mcss.gov.on.ca/en/dshistory/ lifeInstitution/index.aspx*]

So when I was there, I was more a patient needing to be 'fixed' than a human being needing to learn. Not in the description was the abuse that many of us faced daily in those institutions while they were 'fixing' us.

The place was huge. An article by Susan Fisher in the *Ottawa Citizen* on February 25, 1986 (Page B3) said that the institution was built in 1951. She wrote that staff wore *"intimidating uniforms and were addressed by residents as Mr. or Mrs. Parents."*

The 354-acre grounds and school sat on a hill just outside Smiths Falls on County Road 43 (now 3312 Highway 43) "isolating its residents from the rest of the community. Most doors in the building were locked. And many remember Rideau Regional most for its overpowering smell of body odours and disinfectant. As one town resident put it 'you could smell the place for miles around.'"

Susan Ellis, a blogger from Pembroke Ontario [access February 20, 2016: http://susansgonetothebirds.blogspot.ca] writes that the centre included an operating theatre and morgue, full service kitchens, laundry facilities, a bowling alley, a school with a gymnasium and an indoor swimming pool, an 800-seat theatre and dozens of buildings with large wards where patients slept. If you look at an aerial view of the centre you will see a small town with large buildings (four dozen) with even larger institutional buildings for the school and administration. All the buildings are connected by long hallways: the main hallway is a quarter mile long. There are four side hallways that each contain 12 wards and have two stories.

When I was there, over 5,000 meals would have to be prepared three times a day for staff and patients. That's nearly two million meals a year. When my mom came to visit, she and I would go to the staff and visitors dining room to eat. What a difference. They got to pick what they wanted to eat and I am sure that their food tasted better. It was always a big treat to be able to eat there.

Among the staff there were 'babysitters' who watched over us but did not do much for us or with us. There were also electricians, plumbers, maintenance staff, administrators, medical people, teachers, gardeners, and more.

The Centre closed in March 2009. By then it had over 800,000 square feet of building space. That is about the same as 650 houses! In 2011, the centre was bought by a developer to convert it into an active seniors' complex, with athletic facilities and condominiums. It's called the Gallipeau Centre now.

There are several good *Youtube* videos about the centre including a tour after it was closed. Just type in the name of the Rideau Regional Centre and the Gallipeau Centre in the Search box to see these videos. There is also one by me talking about the centre at https://www.youtube.com/watch?v=oKw4bUkemq8.

I helped close the institution. More on that later.

My Time There – Good Times

I had some fun times and also some really bad times at Rideau Regional Centre. Most importantly, I had lots of friends at Rideau. They made it possible to survive. We were, after all, in the same boat.

No matter where you live and what you experience in life, there are usually times when you can find some fun; some enjoyment. It does not mean you want to be there, it just means there are chances to have some good times.

My best memory was the time I got to drive the garbage truck. We had just picked up the garbage and my friend Joe dared me to drive it. I didn't even bump into anything. I never drove before but I had learned how to drive by watching staff. It was a standard transmission and I didn't even stall it. It was fantastic! I never even got in trouble with the staff. When he saw me, he just laughed!

When I was older, me and a bunch of guys would go into town and go shopping at Woolworth's and then go to a movie afterwards. I loved the old westerns like *The Lone Ranger* and *Roy Rogers*.

I worked at various 'placements' at Rideau. I did everything from gardening to serving in the dining halls, to working in the main laundry, to construction work as a plasterer, in the post office and occasional day work.

I enjoyed working on the trucks best. It gave me a sense of freedom in a place where freedom really didn't exist. Driving a garbage truck gave me a power I couldn't get anywhere else. It is good to focus on the good memories. That is where my strength comes from. We want to learn from the bad stuff but not focus on it. When I got out, my life started. I got my driver's license, got a job, got married, and got my own place. That is what is important to remember most days.

I also worked at restaurants in Smiths Falls as temporary staff. All of these places had provided opportunities to work with different people, and learn new skills. But mostly I worked for little money. Many people did not see me as an equal to the paid staff. I didn't care. It got me out of the institution and I was proud of my work.

The work at Rideau may sound somewhat interesting because I did so many different things, but I hated living there. I tried to escape 13 times. That should tell you something.

My Time There – Bad Times

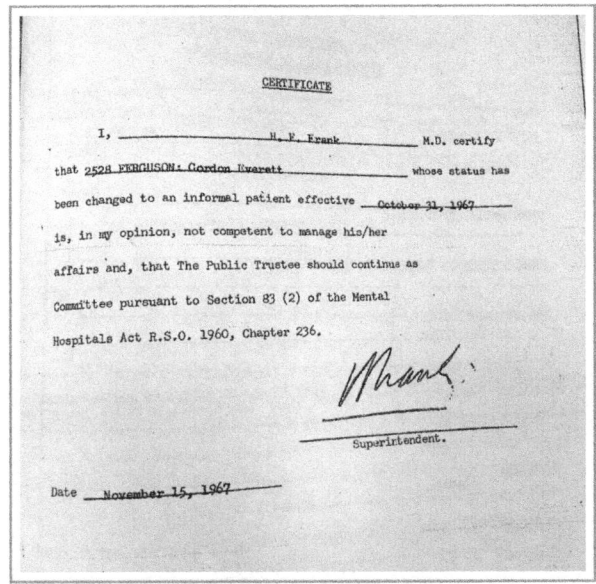

On October 31, 1967, I was declared *"not competent to manage his own affairs."* That paper stayed in my file at Rideau for my whole time there. I was lucky that it did not follow me on discharge in 1974. I lost what little ability I had to make formal decisions about my life. No one should know what that feels like.

Probably everyone who lived there was declared not competent and had the same thing written in their file. We had no rights. It made staff feel more powerful and feel that they were better than us residents. It probably set up a lot of the abuse that we suffered.

Some bad things happened to me at the Rideau Regional Centre. When I was 11 years old, I went home for a visit and my knees were rubbed raw from cleaning the floors with a toothbrush. My mom was mad. She even wrote a letter to Dr Frank.

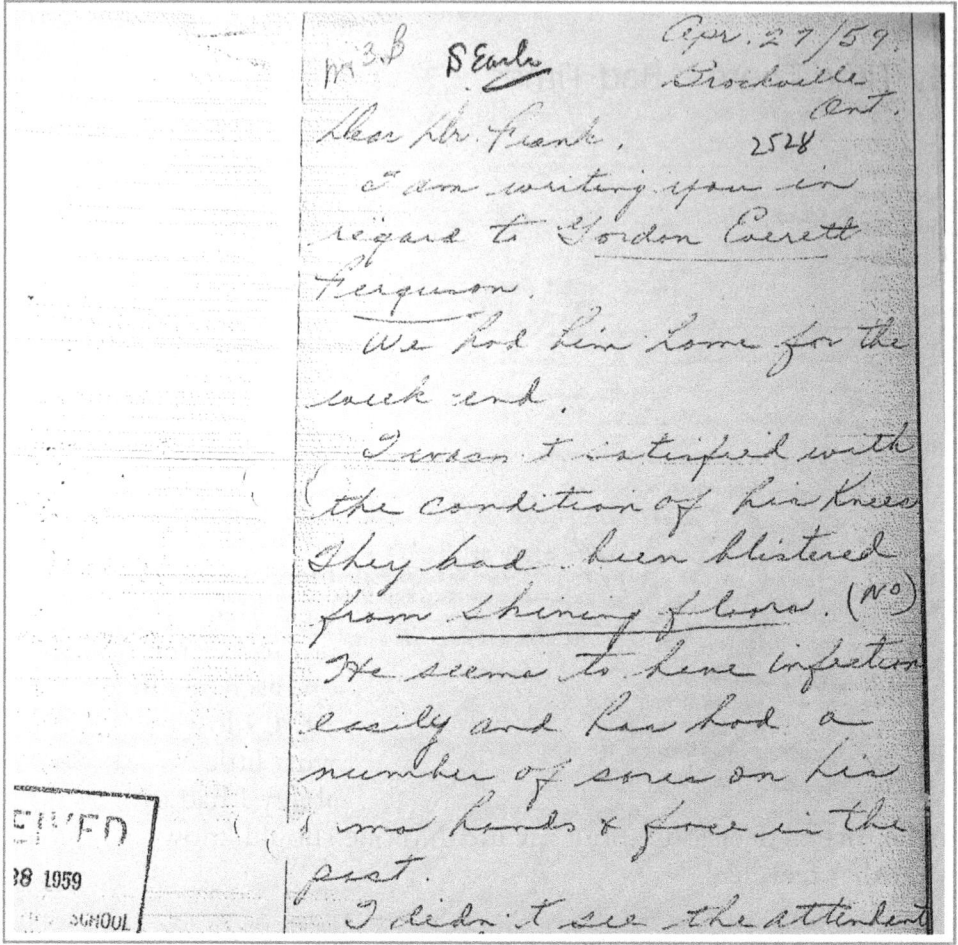

Dear Dr. Frank,

I am writing you in regard to <u>Gordon Everett Ferguson</u>.

We had him home for the weekend.

I wasn't satisfied with the condition of his knees. They had been blistered from <u>shining floors</u>. [Someone wrote (NO) in the margins implying that was not the cause, but it was.] *He seems to have infection easily and has had a number of sores on his hands and face in the past.*

I didn't see the attendant [ends of page 1]

The mean staff worked at night, but not all them were mean. I often had trouble with wetting my bed, and the mean staff thought I was doing it on purpose. In the middle of the night they made me stand in a corner and put the smelly wet bed sheet on my head until the day staff came in. Sometimes they put the stinky sheets in my face forcing me to smell and breathe it. Sometimes they would throw cold water on me.

I was always big and hungry. Sometimes I got called fat. They wanted to put me on a diet but I was always hungry. For a long time, they put me on a 900-calorie-a-day diet. That is not enough food for me! I was always starving! To make it worse they made me work in the dining room. All I could think about was food, looking at other people's food and the delicious smells all around me. I would sneak leftover food off of people's plates and eat it quickly.

One time I got blamed for taking a staff's sandwich. The staff beat the hell out of me, and then put me in a side room for the night. You didn't want to be in a side room, ever.

Sometimes, they would try to embarrass me by making me wear a nightgown for a couple of days, but I didn't care. When I told my mom, she called Dr. Frank to complain.

Sometimes the staff would make me fight other residents. I think that they were betting on who would win. They told me bad things to make me mad and that if I didn't fight the other guy, I would get beat up. The staff would holler and cheer on the fight to keep it going. They would not stop it until the supervisor or head guy came in. In one of these fights, it got really bad, and I put my elbow through a window and cut it. I had to go to the doctor and get stitches. When I came home one weekend with a black eye, my mom asked what happened and I told her that I got in a fight with another patient. I never told her the whole truth. What could she do?

When I was a young teenager the abuse got really bad. I was sexually abused by two male staff. Even today it is very painful to me and I don't like to talk about it. I never told my mom because I was ashamed. Those men made me think it was my fault. I was worried that my mom would get mad at me if she knew. It took me many years before I could tell one of my friends. I think a lot about it today. Those bad memories still turn into nightmares and wake me when I am sleeping.

In those days, the abuse made me run away 13 times! The first time I ran away the staff caught me outside in the middle of the night. I was in trouble for a couple of days. They locked me in a side room and made me wear a nightgown. I had to scrub the ward floor with a toothbrush.

The next time I ran away I got all the way to the Brockville Road in Smiths Falls when a police officer picked me up and brought me back. I guess the staff noticed I was gone and were looking for me.

The police asked me why I ran away but I wouldn't tell him. What was he going to do? I was surrounded by adults who told me I wasn't smart enough to make my own decisions. How could a policeman help against that? For all I knew, he was just like them. When I got back to the ward and I was alone with the staff I was punched in the stomach twice and told not to run away again.

I want to say again that only some of the staff was mean, some were nice.

The best time that I ran away was the time my friend and me wanted to go to Ottawa and get a job. I just walked out the door and told the staff I was going uptown. I got to the highway outside of Smiths Falls and it was snowing. We found an old barn and made a fort in the hay.

When we woke up in the morning there was snow on the ground and we were cold. We had spent the whole night talking and in the morning we decided to go back on our own. After that they tried to separate my buddy and me by putting us in different wards, but we could still get together and talk in the dining room. We fooled them.

I liked school, but I was having problems with the teacher and she would get mad if I didn't do my work. How could I concentrate with everything going on? After a while they told me not to go back and they started to find me jobs around the institution.

One day, we were all cutting up and fooling around, pretending to take spells [seizures] to get the staff going. After we had all faked a few, my friend Caesar took a real one. The staff told him to stop fooling around, got a pail of ice-cold water and threw it at his face when he wouldn't stop. Except that this seizure was a real one.

Caesar died on the floor. His heart stopped. I witnessed my friend die. He wasn't moving. The staff told everyone that he had a seizure and that his heart stopped, but not about the bucket of water. That staff was supposed to be fired but I heard that they brought him back a couple of months later on another ward. It happened on a Sunday night. I had just come back from home. I was very upset. Nobody ever talked to me or asked me what happened.

My first girlfriend was Mary Ann. I liked her hair, and we used to go around the hospital holding hands. She had beautiful brown hair, white skin, and liked the same music as me. We lived on different wards. We would try to find privacy to be together but it was hard. When the staff caught us together they would tell us to stop and separate us.

As I said, I had lots of different jobs at Rideau. I worked in the dining room, kitchen, garbage department, laundry and the post office. One time I found a guy putting up wall tiles. It looked like fun and was really interesting so I asked to work with him. He was a good boss. He showed me what he wanted and how to do it. This was one of my favourite jobs. I have had so many jobs; I am a jack-of-all trades.

I made $22 every 2 weeks for 5 days a week all day or about 25 cents-an-hour. I would spend the money up town, and buy records for my collection.

When I worked in the garden, they would pick us up right after breakfast and we would climb on the back of a truck and be driven to a potato field… there were thousands of hills…. potatoes everywhere. They would bring us back for lunch, and then pick up again and we would work until 5 pm. We pulled weeds with our hands. If someone got tired and refused they would be transferred to another job. But if you refused to do too many jobs you would be called lazy and punished by scrubbing the ward down. If you totally refused all jobs, then they would lock you in the side room.

The whole ward got their hair cut at the same time: a buzz cut like army soldiers got. We all looked the same. I refused to get my hair cut there, and my mom backed me up. She wrote a note telling them that she would look after my haircuts. I would visit a barber on my visits home so I could get my hair cut the way I liked it.

Summer Holidays

I used to spend a lot of time at my Uncle Stanley's farm during my summer vacation. My mom would take me out of Rideau for one month every summer. My cousin Les is the same age as me. I learned to drive a tractor there. *"He's going to wreck that tractor!"* Uncle Stanley yelled, but Les stood up for me and told his dad to give me a chance. The two of them taught me how to drive it. Once the tractor was hooked up to the combine and I drove it! I used to help them with hay and milk the cows.

When I was on my holidays I would spend two weeks with them. My aunt was a great cook, and gave me good meals. They paid me in meals and money for all the work I did. We cleaned the stables by hand. They didn't have any modern equipment, but had a chain in the barn to take out the manure. The farm is still going today, with Les's daughter and her husband running it.

[Gord with cousins Les and Ron]

Sometimes we would play games in the haystacks, hiding and pretending to shoot each other. Once a piece of hay got in my eyeball and another time I jumped out of the haystack and fell hard. Those were the good old days.

The farm was my second home when I lived at Rideau. I would spend my vacation between our house and the farm. My mom had to work, and I was never bored at the farm so I went there a lot. My cousins: Les, Ronnie, and Shirley are like brothers and a sister to me.

My dad was a nice man and I have his name as my middle name. He was a foreman on the water main repair crew for the Brockville Public Utilities Company.

My favourite memory of Dad is when we went partridge hunting. I had a .22 rifle in my hand and I tried to shoot two partridges, but I missed them both. My dad shot four of them that day. We had a good supper. My Dad laughed and encouraged me. "*I brought you hunting, and you missed two. Keep on trying.*"

After that I borrowed my friend's .410 shotgun, and I practiced shooting at a can until I could put a hole in it. I went partridge hunting twice more after that. I tried to train two dogs to be hunting dogs, but when I let them off the leash they both ran back to the camp.

I also spent time at the cottage. I remember so well getting up early in the mornings, hopping into the boat to go out fishing, catching some fish, cleaning them and then cooking them up. Such fun.

I also learned to ride my bike at cousin Shirley's home. Such independence to be able to ride a bike so much faster than I could walk or run. I didn't experience such freedom again until I got my driver's licence and my own car.

Shirley reminded me that I once came to her rescue. Given the life that I was living at the Rideau Regional Centre, I understood what it felt like to be picked on. Shirley, her brothers and I were out swimming in the lake one day during a summer holiday. One of her brothers was fooling around and held her head under water. I rescued her by pulling him off of her. It felt good to help her. Helping others is something I've tried to do all of my life.

Leaving Rideau Regional Centre

I said that we can learn from the bad times. My last lesson at Rideau was about how to get out.

I got myself out in 1974 when I was 26. I kept telling them I wanted to leave and even found myself a job at the Skyline Hotel in Brockville. It wasn't until my mom phoned the hospital and wrote them a letter to tell them that I got a job that they listened.

In a report from a senior person at Rideau it said, *"In March of 1974 Gordie had the opportunity of living at home with his parents in Brockville and working at the Skyline Hotel. All reports received have been favourable and indicate that his work is satisfactory. He is to be discharged effective October 25, 1974."*

[Gord in his 30s]

You can see that for seven months they let me 'try' to live at home and 'try' having a job, but I was still officially a resident of Rideau. It was only when they were satisfied with how things were going for me, that they 'discharged' me. You will notice that nowhere does it say that I was the one asking to leave Rideau or what I thought about living at home and working. It was not up to me. That's just wrong.

When I was discharged, I could not sign for myself because of that 'incompetent' document in my file. I was allowed to sign a permission form for Rideau to release information about me – but not my own discharge papers.

After I was discharged from Rideau I did work in the food services at the Skyline Hotel. I also worked at a couple of local restaurants. I worked at the Brockville Community Workshop and the Brockville Psychiatric Hospital as a work placement as well.

There is no place in modern society for institutions where you put together hundreds or thousands of people. Part of my advocacy work after leaving Rideau was to help close it and other institutions down. The other part was to try and make sure that old or new institutions were not opened.

Sadly, we are now using nursing homes as places where young and older people with disabilities are being sent because we have not figured out how to keep them at home. It is horrible. It is not right. We have to keep on fighting. It is tiring. But if we don't do it, we will lose our voice again. We know what happens when we don't speak up and fight for the same rights that everyone else has. Nursing homes are just another institution.

Chapter 4   Getting a Life

Earning My Driver's License

Like I said, I was discharged in 1974 when I was 26 years old and I went to work at the Skyline Hotel. I saved some money and bought my first car for $500. It was my "Black Rambler." It ran really well. I had it for a year and then I sold it and bought my "Blue Nova."

[Gord cleaning his "Blue Nova"]

I had a few fender benders in all my cars. My last car was a 1976 "Red Sunbird" with a black roof. My Sunbird was my favourite car. It saved my life when I was in an accident with it. I came home late one night when I should have stayed in Smiths Falls and slept in the car, but instead I went into the ditch and the Sunbird saved me.

I stopped driving when I had glaucoma and the doctor said I couldn't drive anymore. That was hard. It is hard to lose your freedom when you can't drive. You are always dependent on other people. I sure miss my cars.

The best part of having a car? I met the love of my life at the old Brockville Community Workshop. Donna liked my car and me. Most people remember dates driving their very own car. These are special memories.

Donna and I Marry On June 24, 1989

I met Donna when we both worked at the Brockville Community Workshop. We started hanging around at lunchtime. I liked how small, funny, friendly and happy she was. I was living with my mom and Donna was living with a roommate being supported by an agency. I wanted to marry her, because I loved her and I wanted to move out of my mom's house.

One night I went over to her apartment and her roommate was there. I got down on my knee, pulled out a ring, and asked her, "Will you marry me?" She said yes and then kissed me. Then she screamed and danced all around the room. Actually we were both screaming and dancing. We then had to tell her family. They were happy for us.

We started living together right away. On June 24, 1989 (over 26 years ago now) I married Donna. What an amazing day. What an amazing woman. She is the love of my life. We bring each other out of a bad mood. She is funny; she loves to party. Donna makes me happy when I see her. We tease each other. We call each other cute names. We are lucky to have found each other.

[Gord's mother, Audrey, Donna and Gord]

We had lots of fun buying things that we needed. I got a credit card. We bought fast food everyday and then I started collecting things. I bought lots of baseball cards, records and movies. Today I have over 2000 records and baseball cards. It worked well because we got along. Once in a while we had arguments but we were able to solve them.

Our first apartment was in a nice apartment building in Brockville until my mom asked us to come live with her and help her share the bills. So Donna and I moved in with her at her house on Chislett Street.

Friends

[Enjoying a beautiful summer day with some of my friends. Left to right: Gord, Donna, Doug Cartan, John Hickling, Rick Trapp, and Sandy Gray]

It's funny when you meet people; you never know when they will show up in your life again. I worked as a dishwasher at several places in Brockville. I liked working in the kitchen and I was good at it. They were hot jobs but I was used to it a bit from working at the Rideau dining room. I also worked at the Psychiatric Hospital as a porter.

When I worked at the Skyline Hotel in the 1970's I met two co-workers: Rita and Kathy. About 30 years later both Kathy and Rita worked for BDACI where I am a board member. It is wonderful how people keep coming back into your life.

Kathy wrote to me about first meeting me: *"I remember when we first met, we both worked at the then Skyline Hotel. We always shared a smile when I passed through the kitchen. My first impression of you was that of a gentle person. Who knew that for 25 plus years later we would again journey together in our lives?*

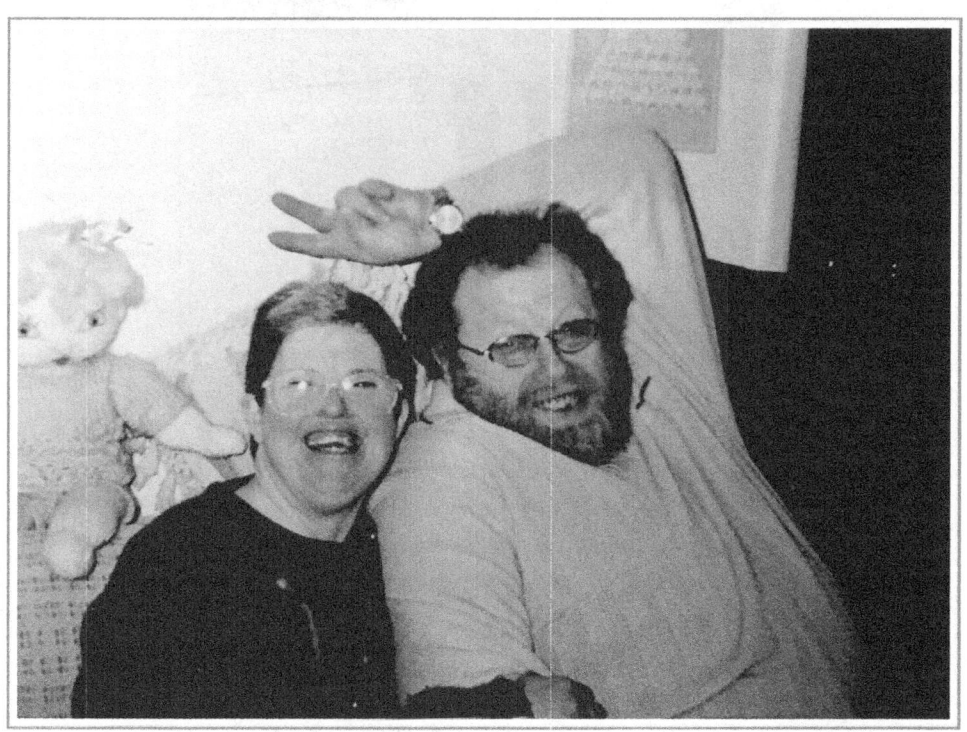

[Donna and Gordon enjoying their home.]

[Donna dancing at our 25th anniversary party]

"We crossed paths again when I joined the board at BDACI. I remember you on the board as a person who listened intently, you don't share often in meetings but when you do the wisdom you provided comes from a place of deep thought or personal experience. You always remind us of what is important."

Kathy has told me that she admires my "ability to overcome…. You take things as they come, are thoughtful about them and calmly devise a plan to persevere. This is a trait that I admire in you. I also think about your infectious giggle, and great sense of humour."

Kathy is no longer a board member. Today she is a coordinator at BDACI. In the last year or so she is one of the people that have taken me on trips to the hospital in Kingston. We sang Meatloaf's *Bat out of Hell* song. As she tells me, *"I will never listen to that song again without thinking of what a positive attitude you have about the cancer. Thank you for that Gordon."*

Kathy describes Donna as a *"firecracker -- always sizzling with energy and ready for the next exciting adventure."* She understands that Donna's qualities were what attracted me to her all those years ago. This little woman is bigger than life and has the ability to make me smile and be inspired to take on life and laugh at it when it doesn't go as planned.

Kathy wrote me a really lovely letter in which she said, *"As for you and Donna, well what a gift to be in your presence, watching how loving and playful the two of you are with each other. You love without shyness and show this love for one another no matter who is in the room. I have learned from you two that there is no right or wrong way to show affection for our partner and we should take advantage of each and every opportunity to show one another our love."*

The Fergusons and Friends
2nd annual
Neighbourhood Carol Sing
December 17, 6pm

Followed by hot chocolate and cookies
Please join us
At The Fergusons - 364 Church Street

[Annual Ferguson & Friends Neighbourhood Carolling Party.
Left to right: Val and Robert Wykes, Dieter Reinhardt, Kathy Senneker, Joel Blackwell,
Gord, Donna, Nanne Reinhardt, Caroline Brown, Laurelle Avery]

Brockville and District Association for Community Involvement (BDACI)

I joined the board of the Brockville and District Association for Community Involvement in 1991, two years after my marriage. I was on the Civitan Club Board before that for about four years or so.

I love BDACI. I always wanted to be on the board – to do something to help people. I also wanted to keep learning. Through BDACI and other advocacy work I was able to do

other things like go to conferences. I have been to lots of
conferences and I always learn something new when I go. I
chose BDACI because I liked the people. I went to meetings
before I went on the board. The people were nice and I
agreed with what they were doing. I went downtown to see
Doug Cartan, the Executive Director then, to see how I
could join the board. Dianne Hickling, recommended that I
sit as a director.

[May 2006 BDACI Board — left to right: Audrey Cole,
Pat Lacasse, Gord, Harry Pott, Tim Utting,
Nancy McNamara, Suzanne Dumas and Dianne Hickling]

Dianne thought that someone with a disability needed to be
on the board. She and I have worked together on many
committees and also on the board. This is how she describes
us working together to other people: "I think what stands
out for me, is that Gord doesn't have a lot to say at meetings
but you can tell his mind is always working when he is sitting
there. He is listening, understanding and hearing everything,

and I have always been impressed by the fact that when he does speak up, he will make a statement that hits you – it will be profound.

"Gord usually sits to the right of me in the meetings, and I feel his presence to keep me grounded to know that he is there and fully participating and comes up with some brilliant things.

"We have known Gord and Donna for years. I didn't get to know Gord well until he became involved with the board. I have always appreciated having him on the board, and his ideas. It is always fascinating to hear about all the things that People First (a self-advocacy group that Gord started in Brockville) have been involved with here. That whole dynamic is incredible and what Gord has done is so impressive.

"I consider Gord and Donna friends and workmates. Gord has broken barriers in his life. He and Donna getting married broke a barrier. Being married 25 years is more than a lot of people can do these days. What an accomplishment. Gord's life has been so impressive. What he has done and what he has accomplished.

"For me personally it has been a journey knowing Gord, and always learning. He is always teaching one way or another. I would be lost without him sitting on that side of me at meetings. He has always been a teacher, in so many ways. He has taught so many people in so many ways. Gord has taught so many of us to increase our expectations. I am always astounded at the things that he says, and his memory. Gord your memory drives me crazy!"

I've been involved with BDACI ever since. This year will be 25 years. Who would have thought that a kid who grew up in an institution would one day be a board member of an organization with thoughtful Executive Directors, board members, staff and their families all working together to make all of our lives better.

It was easier for me at BDACI when I had eyesight and I could read all the notes. Now the other board members and my support workers read the minutes out loud to me before the meetings so that I will know what is in them.

[Harry Pott, President of BDACI, presenting Gord with the Community Involvement Award, 2000. Also pictured is Donna]

Harry Pott was a board member in the 90's. He wrote about what he learned from and about me during some drives together to Toronto: *"During those trips I learned more about what he was thinking about all kinds of things than I ever learned about him at a board meeting. It is easier to talk in a vehicle. When there are other people in a meeting saying things that are right, Gord doesn't need to talk, but when there isn't anyone else saying it, he is very clear about what his principles and values are. You embrace that. That is what it takes for Gord to say what is going on his head. As long as other people are talking, he doesn't need to say something, but if you say something that he doesn't agree with he will let you know. And it is usually profound. That's the making of 'Gord's advocacy gene' – community contribution. Gord becomes involved with an organization that is trying to do good in the community, rather than expecting the community to always do stuff for you. You give back by becoming involved with a group like that."*

[Left to right: Gord, Paul Young (President of People First Canada), Donna and Beth French]

In February of 2016, my dear friend Beth French, the current Executive Director, died unexpectedly. I was on the committee that hired her. She was my friend for many years and a big supporter of Donna and me. She made it possible for me to write this book and for BDACI to help publish it. She was much too young – like me. People like her make it possible for me to be me. She understood me. When she did not understand something, she asked. She used to visit me in my home and we would have coffee and a chat regularly to make sure that Donna and I were doing well. She always wanted to make sure that other people saw us in the best light possible. It makes me so sad to think that she will never read my book. People like her should never die – they have too many gifts to offer.

The Band!

In the 80's *Crackers* was my favourite band to see in concert. Reg Denis and his wife Patti Warden are the leads of the band and having been making music together for over 45 years. Based in Hamilton, where Reg is First Vice-President of Local 293 of the Hamilton Musicians Guild, they toured around Canada and the U.S.A. for years including lots of stops in the Brockville area. They were regulars at the El Macombo, in Toronto where the Rolling Stones often rehearse before their new tours.

Reg remembers how I used to come out to all their band's shows whenever they were in town. He wrote: *"Gord was always there waiting for us as we drove into the venue and his eyes lit up when he saw our tour bus. Gord would often help us unload and set up our gear or carry our luggage to the rooms which helped us a lot, and we shared many a soda together.*

"We enjoyed seeing him take pictures during our shows with his new camera and we'd often go to eat across the street from the local hotel together.

"The whole band enjoyed all the jokes, antics and laughter we shared, but none enjoyed this more then good ole Gord. Gord just seemed to love our company as much as we did his and I would buy his meals in return for his help.

"Gord and I sometimes drove around town together for outings as I would shop for things I needed and he enjoyed sharing these road trips with me.

"We all love Gord and always will as we fondly recall our memorable times together. May God bless our close pal Gord and keep him as happy as he always was whenever we would meet. We'll meet again, don't know where and don't know when, but we'll meet again, some sunny day. ROCK ON GORD! XOX"

[Gord on stage with Reg Denis]

[Gord singing duet with Reg]

A few times they even let me go up on the stage and I sang with them! They were definitely my favourite band back in those days. Reg and Patti have told me that they think of me as a kind, loyal, considerate, helpful and loving man who loves music, life, laughter and all his great friends. Right back at you!

[Gord gets a kiss from Patti Warden.]

Chapter 5   Owning Our Own House

The First Homes

Like I already said, Donna and I had our own apartment until
my mom asked us to live with her and help her share the
bills. She lived in a small house on Chislett Street and soon
we decided to buy a bigger house together at 49 Orchard
Street in Brockville. Donna, Mom and I were all joint owners
of the house. This was the first house that I ever owned.
Donna and I were so proud.

For nine years, from 1998 until 2007, Donna and I lived with
my mother in that house. The mortgage was held by all three
of us.

Beth French remembered visiting us at Orchard Street: *"Even though he was disagreeing with some of his mother's decisions, they did have a very strong partnership. I spent a fair amount of time with all three of them in the years when they were proud homeowners. I often went for tea with them and they would proudly talk about how they bought the house, what a collaborative effort it was, and what a help they were to each other. Audrey and Donna had a very good relationship. Gord and his mom sometimes had a volatile relationship, but ultimately they had made a commitment to each other, to live together and to support each other because it was a better way of life for all three of them. I thought that was a very positive message. It wasn't about Audrey making sacrifices and supporting Gord and Donna. It was about Gord and Donna making a very direct and concrete contribution to Audrey's well being also. Audrey would be the first person to acknowledge that."*

[Gord doing dishes]

In 2006 I started to slowly lose my sight and we knew it would get harder and harder for me to use the steps outside to get into the house. It would become soon too dangerous for me and my Mom was also getting older. So for accessibility reasons, we needed to sell our home in January 2007. Mom purchased the house at 364 Church Street on her own. My mom convinced Donna and I to give up our rights as property owners. She said she had a better plan. We trusted her. How could we do anything else? It was so very difficult for us to do give up our house. Home ownership is one of the most valued roles in our community. To give it up meant taking a big step backward. It was so hard.

Mom's Plan for Us

Mom talked with someone who gave her the idea of selling the house and creating a trust for Donna and me. I wish she never got that advice.

She thought that when she died the house should be sold and Donna and I would go to a nursing home. She tried to convince us that this was a good idea. This made me very angry and Mom and I had lots of arguments about it. She knew that a nursing home is just a smaller institution and that I had enough of institutions.

Mom and I had really bad arguments and I would get so mad that she wouldn't listen to me that I would yell at her, and slam doors. The next day, mom would tell everyone that I was angry and that I had a behaviour problem. She never told anyone about why I was mad, just that I got angry. People thought I was being difficult.

Finally we got Maggie (our dog) who was the peacekeeper. Maggie calmed us all down a bit.

When I think back, the first few years of the new decade were very hard for Donna and me. Donna was diagnosed with Alzheimer's Disease in 2010.

My mom and I continued to fight about the house and her plans for us. Finally, I just got tired of arguing with Mom, because she wasn't going to change her mind. I stopped arguing and then I started worrying inside.

In April 2010 I got really sick. All that worry caused me to get sick. It is not good to keep pain and hurt inside. It eats you up. I was delirious for a time and had to be hospitalized at a psychiatric hospital for one month. The doctors said that I had an untreated infection that led to the delirium. Most of my vision was now gone. I was worried about the future. It was all too much.

Because I can't see, I couldn't find the washroom in the hospital, so I had lots of accidents. Soon they had me in diapers, and strapped me in a chair since they didn't want me walking around bumping into things or falling. All I could think about was wanting to go home. My mom and Donna came to visit me, but I kept telling them I wanted to go home. I wasn't sure I was ever going to go home again. I can't tell you how frightening that month was. Each day lasted forever. People don't understand how frightened I was.

It was all too much. How do you cope with so much tragedy and bad news at one time? If it wasn't for Donna's love and energy, and the support of other family and friends, I don't know what would have happened. It really was just too much.

Mom's Death in 2011

But I did go home from the hospital. A year later my mom died on September 9, 2011 – one day before my 63rd birthday.

Caroline Brown, one of my support workers said, *"Before Audrey died, I felt like Gord's assistant. I really enjoyed that role because Gord is a hero of mine. Once Audrey passed away, the role changed to more personal care and meal making etc. Gord got a few male workers and I started working more with Donna. Gord set his sights on what he wanted and went for it, fortunately he had lots of support to help him through it. Today Gord is very content and satisfied about how it went. He used to travel a lot with all his advocacy work and that has given him even more confidence to be an example to other people. He knows his roles and he lives them. Gord is in his glory in his home with his wife."*

My mom made a plan of what she wanted for Donna and me and put it into her Will. Funny though, this plan was not what she wanted for herself. She didn't want to go to the nursing home herself. She wanted to live out her life at home.

Mom was very clear with her instructions to the trustees that Donna and I must move to a nursing home upon her death. She thought a nursing home would be the safest place for us to live. I don't think that she could figure out how we could live in our home.

My mom's Will told the trustees to make sure that Donna and I would receive the financial support we needed. We were her only beneficiaries. All of her property (including the house) was to be sold and placed in a trust for us.

While the trustees were given "absolute discretion," they promised to ensure that we would be well cared for. If we died before the trust money was spent, then they got to keep any leftover money.

Fighting for Our Home

I think that the trustees were worried about how they were going to look after Donna and my needs. That's why they supported my mom's plan. I want this book to be a bridge back to them. They did what they thought was best and now that everything is settled I'm just glad that they are back in my life again. They are really good people.

It took two years to fight to save my house. When my mom died the first thing I asked my staff was, "What's going to happen to Donna and me?" I was worried and scared and I knew that I was in for a big fight.

I talked to everyone I could find. It was important to get people to help me and I knew that I couldn't do it all by myself.

The trustees were only doing what my mom asked them to do. They meant well and thought they were doing what was best for us. So they tried their best to convince Donna and me to move. We had lots of meetings to try to work out a solution. Donna and I even agreed to visit two nursing homes so that "we could see if we would like to live there."

The nursing home in Athens seemed very nice and friendly, and seemed like a nice place to visit, but we didn't want to live there. I told them that I might move there "maybe later, when I get older." I was using my peace-making skills.

When that didn't work, the trustees hired a lawyer to try to force me to go. After a while, my supporters and I realized that I had to hire a lawyer too.

So I hired an Ottawa lawyer on December 14, 2011. The first thing our lawyer told me to do was to take a competency test. She said that she thought the trustees would force me to do it anyway. She said that if I volunteered to take it I would have more control. If I passed the tests, then my case would be very strong. If I didn't pass them, then I could have a say in who would make decisions for me.

I PASSED ALL FOUR COMPETENCY TESTS!!! January 18, 2012 was a big day. Dr. Clarissa Bush declared me

capable to make decisions regarding all aspects of my personal care and property. She also declared that I was capable of making a power of attorney for both personal care and finances for that time when I might become incapable of deciding for myself because of illness or injury – just like every other Canadian should do.

A year later, the (January 7, 2013) the trustees of my mother's estate and I agreed to an understanding in which Donna and I would continue to live in our home and the house would be transferred into my name. The only condition was that I had to get a mortgage to pay for the trustee's lawyer and take over my mom's line of credit – about $50,000 in total.

BDACI also made a guarantee to the trustees that they would give Donna and I the support we needed for day-to-day living. That made a big difference.

We went to lots of banks and credit unions and even reverse mortgage companies. Everywhere was the same story. I qualified, but because of Donna's disability she couldn't sign the mortgage. The problem was that the home was her "matrimonial" home. She had rights and we wanted to protect those rights. We did not want her to be declared incompetent. That was very important for her and very important to me.

Everything was taking so long – so many meetings, so many conversations. It took us another 8 months (until August 7, 2013) to work this out. Just when I was ready to give up, five of our friends came together and offered us $50,000 loan. Donna and I live on a government pension and we don't have a lot of extra money. Our friends said that we only had to pay them back when we sold the house. What a great offer! That was one of the best days of my life!

A month later on my 65th birthday (September 10, 2013) we had a big party to thank all of our supporters. I finally had my own home that Donna and I can share for as long as we live. A home where we control the temperature, we control where we sleep and what we eat. We control who visits and who does not. A home where we can live as a married couple supported by BDACI to live a full and rich life and supported by family and friends who love us and who we love. It took a long time – but it was worth it. We have achieved what most Canadians take for granted – a family home in a house of our choosing.

[Gord and Donna's "We are homeowners
and Gord's 65th birthday party."]

[Donna spent a lot of time making birdhouses
to thank their supporters for their help.]

Chapter 6   The Role of Long-Term Relationships

When you read my stories, you will notice that it is the long-term relationships in my life, that define my life. First of all, of course, there was my relationship with my Mom.

[Gord and his mom, Audrey]

My Aunt Jean described our relationship, *"Audrey was proud of anything that Gord ever did. She was proud of him driving a car. Gord drove to Toronto for Gord's Uncle Carl and Aunt Dorothy's anniversary. Audrey didn't want to drive so Gord did. Gord got a job washing dishes. Gord did woodworking. He made chairs. Gord was very good at woodworking. Gord was also good at electronics. She was very proud when he got married, and got his driver's licence. Audrey was always there when Gord needed her. She went up to Toronto when Gord was diagnosed with cancer for the first time. Gord did fantastic. Gord was treated with chemotherapy and surgery. Nothing held him back. Gord doesn't feel sorry for himself. He has never let anything hold him back. He even learned to write with his other hand after he lost his fingers."*

[Gord's cousins and friends attending Gord and Donna's
25th anniversary party. Left to right: Fred & Pat Allport, Nancy Purvis,
Nancy Webster, Harry Purvis, Ann & Ron Bryan sitting.]

[Gord's cousins attending Gord and Donna's 25th anniversary party:
Left to right: Marilyn Gibson, Amanda Fenlong,
Mackenzie Horbay, and Marion Gibson.]

[Donna chatting with Gord's cousins at their 25th anniversary.]

My Aunt Jean also reminded me that my mother and I had a lot in common. Aunt Jean said that every time she saw my mother and me it was always the same, a big hug and welcome.

Aunt Jean said that I am very determined and will find a way out of most problems. *"I stayed at Audrey's house for about a month when I was about to give birth to my daughter, so I got to see them during normal days together. Gord is a lot like Audrey. She would never give up. She would do anything. She did electrical work, plumbing, flooring, anything at all. She had the most beautiful flower garden at her other house. She and Gord built the pond. She could do anything when she put her mind to it. Gord has a great memory, he has courage and determination. I remember Gord at a family reunion and he never mentioned his problems. He just has a great attitude just like his mom. He takes after his mom a lot. Don't ever quit. Audrey loved her son, as much as he loved her."*

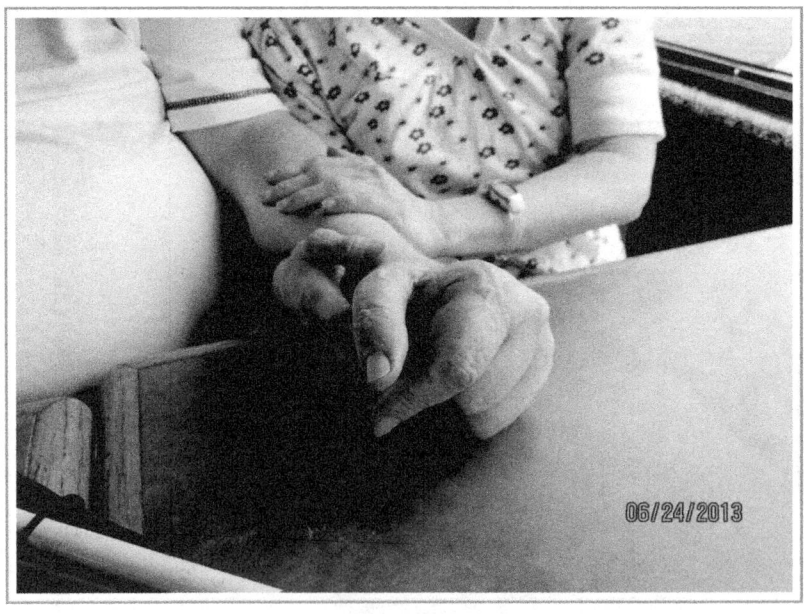

Then there is my relationship with Donna of over 25 years. Like I already said, Donna is the love of my life. She is my sweetheart, my wife, my partner and I love her. She needs me. Donna was the most beautiful woman in the world when I could see her face.

[25th Anniversary Dance]

The many friends I have made and kept over many decades through my advocacy work, and my hobbies. I have been friends with many of these people for more than 30 years.

My cousins, Ron and Shirley are like a brother and sister to me.

[Cousin Ron with Gord]

Also very important are my relationships with the board members, staff, peers and their families at BDACI. Like I already have said, I have been on the board for 25 years now.

As you can see, all of these relationships have lasted 25 or more years. Together, everyone has helped me get to where I am now, just like we have helped other people. That is what living in a community really means. It's a give and take. Sometimes you can give help and sometimes you need help. Getting to know people and being part of the community means that you have more options.

[Installation of the 2015 BDACI Board of Directors: left to right — Gord, Jane Barken, Mark Primeau, Sam Peters, Kristi Carter, Nancy McNamara, Chris Eady, Cathie Blair. Not shown: Christine Reitsma and Bobbi Stephen.]

Doug Cartan wrote me the following note recently: *"I wouldn't have met you if it wasn't for your role on the Board of Directors of BDACI. Rick Trapp wouldn't have met you if it weren't for your role on the board. Dianne Hickling might not have stayed in touch with you if it wasn't for your role on the board.*

"I think the people that are around you right now are there because of our relationship with you over the years, not as People First or the advocacy work you do but more as you were a fellow director. You are one of the longest serving directors. You were on the board the whole ten years I was executive director of BDACI. We sat on some of the committees together. That's where our relationship formed.

"You were the chair of the General Association. It is not a small thing that your role on the board strengthened the important relationships that have continued for so many years. Long-term involvement in important things builds bonds that last a lifetime. People who have common

interests tend to stay. It was all those years of relationship with us, me, Rick Trapp, and Harry Pott.

"Rick was president in 1998 when I left. He is still around. It is about being around on a constant basis, and having a common interest/ passion. You are so passionate about your work that people can identify with that. One of the things that we learned in our work was that importance of long-term relationships."

[As Chair of the General Association Committee, Gord gives his report as the Exective Director, Doug Cartan, looks on.]

The relationship I have with Doug has been so important in my life. I remember offering to drive Doug home after a board meeting once. I think he was surprised that I had a license, and even more surprised that I had a car. (He didn't have one in those days) I always enjoyed watching people's reactions when I drove my car – it was not what they expected and that was fun to watch.

[Gord gives his report as Cathie Blair, President, joins in.]

Beth French said that, *"The fact that Gord had relationships that were substantive enough to provide him with an alternative to his mom's plan is the most remarkable lesson of the story. His personality is a factor in establishing those relationships. His efforts on behalf of the organization was acknowledged, he contributed over a significant period of time, not just dabbled, went on the record. I think that the people who knew him well, honestly respected that contribution and felt that it was essential that they play a part in helping him get what he wanted and needed in the end. So I think that the extent of the relationships is an important lesson."*

Dianne Hickling wrote, *"It is interesting that Gord's mom and my mom were good friends. I didn't know Gord growing up, but my sister worked at the college with Donna and they became good friends. Today she is on Facebook with Gord and Donna. There has been a connection for many years."*

[Left to right: Gord, Doug Mather and Gerald MacAfee]

Long-term relationships are more important than the work
we do, the things we own, and even more important than
good health. We can lose all of those things quickly. It is the
people we love and who love us that help all of us do well in
life.

Hobbies

Around 2008, when Donna and I were still living with my
mom, Caroline Brown (one of my workers) asked me what I
wanted to do with our time together. I told her I wanted to
organize my music collection. My collections are very
important to me. For many years when I lived in the
institution, nothing was mine. If I had something nice then
other people would take it or it would suddenly get lost. I

was not allowed to own a lot of things and what I did own was often searched through by staff to make sure that I didn't have something I wasn't allowed to have. Nobody can do that to me now. It took me many years of collecting to make my collections so big. I am so proud of my collections.

It took Caroline and me the whole summer to organize my music. I have over 1,000 45's records and even some 78's. For example, I have the original Gene Autry *Rudolf the Red Nosed Reindeer* on a 78! Then there are the many hundreds of full-length albums. There isn't a band that I don't have at least one album of in my collection.

[Gord and Caroline Brown organize his record collection]

I used to go around to garage sales, and auction sales. If I saw records, I would put them all together and make a deal on them. I also bought them at record stores. When I worked on the garbage truck at Rideau we used to drive by the old record store, and I would find lots. I used to get half of my 45's out of the RCA-Victor factory. This is when I started collecting them. They would throw away good records so I took them. I wanted them all. I like all kinds of music. My favourite band was the Beatles. I spent a lot of time listening to my music. I have some really good records, for instance I have a gold vinyl Elvis Presley record and lots of coloured vinyl records. It makes me happy to have them in my home. Caroline helped me a lot over the years I appreciate her work and what she has done for me.

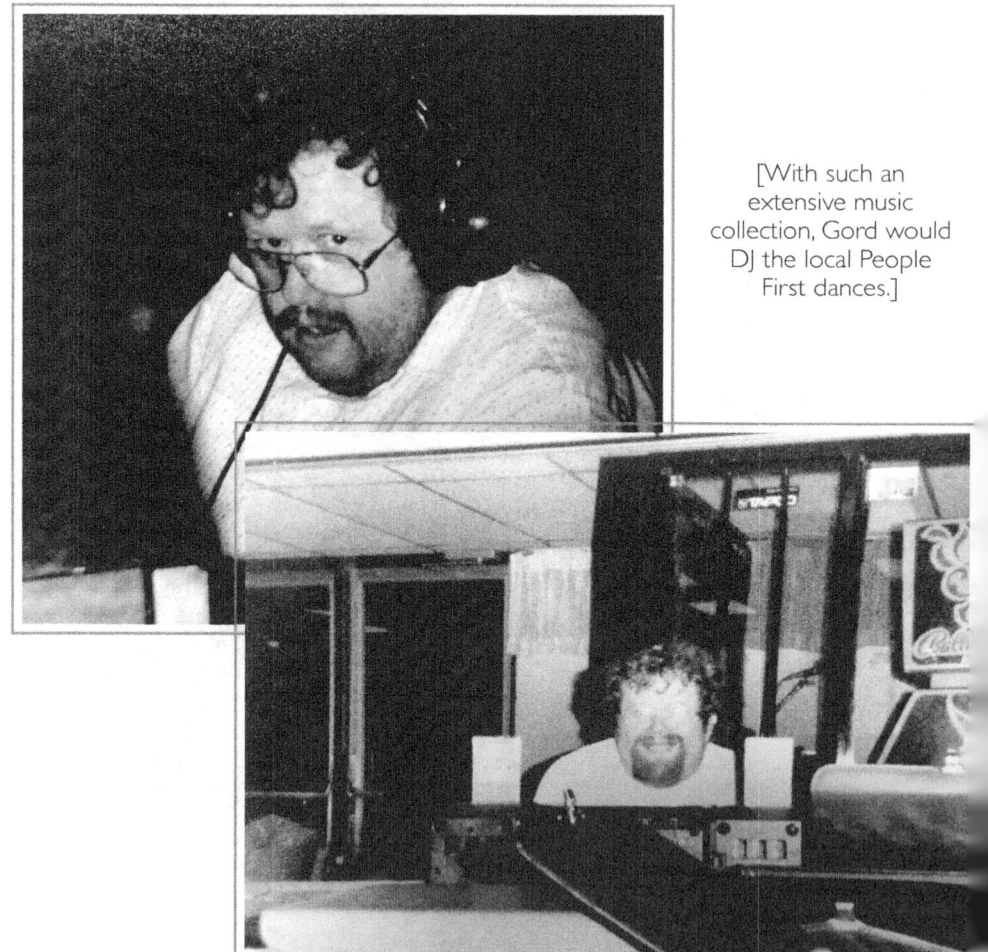

[With such an extensive music collection, Gord would DJ the local People First dances.]

But, my favourite collection is my sports cards. I used to read the back of the cards and memorize all the stats about the players. I know lots of things about all of the players. I have thousands of cards: Baseball and hockey. I even have some rare cards like Babe Ruth and Wayne Gretzky.

At one time, my mom thought I had too many cards. She told me to throw some out. I couldn't do that. These cards were too important to me. Instead I starting hiding them in places where she couldn't find them like above the drop ceiling in the basement. I also have my beta and VHS movies. It has taken me decades to collect these special things in my life. They represent that I can do what I want. I own them. I don't want to sell them. I don't even want to know how much they're worth.

Chapter 7   Brockville and District Association for Community Involvement (BDACI)

[Left to right: Nancy Oliver, Pamela Kirkland, Nancy McNamara, Pat Lacasse, Gord and Beth French outside the BDACI offices on King Street.]

Although I was a board member of BDACI, I did not receive formal home supports from them until 2004. Before that Donna and I managed on our own with the help of my family. In the beginning BDACI, hired a support worker for 5 hours per week to help Donna, my mom and me around the house and to help me with my advocacy work. I had started to lose my vision and things were getting tough for me to figure out.

It is so important to have a very friendly organization filled with people who knew what I had gone through at the Rideau – a group who knew about my roles in the community, my financial difficulties, and my relationships with Donna and my mom. A group of people who had a vision of what Donna and me could do and encouraged us to be active. A group of people who could offer me the supports that continues to help us through all of the good times in our lives and the bad times.

Life can be overwhelming. There are so many things to juggle at one time. I am very competent at many things, just like you. But I am not able to do everything at once, just like you too, I think. Who doesn't need help from family, friends and community supports?

[Donna, Audrey Cole, and Gord.]

Throughout the last dozen years, people at BDACI have helped Donna and me with many aspects of our lives. If it wasn't for these people, we might well have ended up in a nursing home like my mother wanted.

One of the things BDACI did for us was to help Donna and me with our important volunteer jobs. Donna, volunteers at the hospital and exercises at the YMCA by going to aqua fit where she made a good friend, Joanne.

I am a board member of several organizations, including BDACI itself. It takes a lot to be a board member. When I go to the meetings themselves I have to think and talk about the important issues.

Just the daily things of living like preparing meals, housekeeping, laundry, grocery shopping, personal hygiene, paying bills, home maintenance, shopping, and so much more all need time and effort. Our support workers, that BDACI helps us hire and supervise, provide us with that daily support.

We also used to have a more active social life before we both got ill. When we feel well we want to get out and do things. We often go shopping, swimming, the movies, concerts, hockey games or visit friends. Without that help we might live in the community but we would not be part of our community.

There are larger things in our lives that need support as well. We needed to make long-term plans for our life together. We needed people to help us think about issues to make good decisions. We need to plan for a good future so we don't end up in a nursing home. We need help to think about all the complicated rules about support. We need to get more government funding and community supports.

Money is always such an important and frustrating part of life for most Canadians. Our income almost never meets our needs. I'm not talking about having money so that we can take a vacation to some fancy place, or to build a big house, or to buy lots of expensive furniture. We just want our home, a place to work, enough money to buy food and home repairs – that sort of thing.

BDACI also helped us in another big way. They came up with a creative mortgage idea when the banks turned me down, helped us tell our story and then ask our friends for a $50,000 loan. Not many groups will take the time or make the effort to do that. They understood how important owning our house was for us and they committed to helping us do it. They had to learn all sorts of new things to help us get our home. They had no experience in helping people own their own homes before. They did all of this for Donna and me. We are so grateful.

Friendly Support Workers

We need both paid and unpaid support. I have already talked a lot about my unpaid support… my friends, so I will talk about my staff now.

This one is very tricky. No matter how much we talk about this, it always is confusing to everyone. That makes it very important.

I hire only the best staff to support Donna and me. My staff are fantastic. This means that they are kind, caring, respectful, and share our interests. They spend a lot of time with us in our home and as a result we get very close to them. But remember I said that I hired them, so this also means that they are working when they are here with us. Most people have to work for money, so if I didn't hire them, then we wouldn't have met them and they would have to go somewhere else to work. We wouldn't be able to see them as much as we do now. Because we are so close, they feel like friends and family and sometimes we even get to meet their friends and their families.

But this is a real tricky problem for both my staff and us. Our staff like us and want to be friendly and kind to us. We really like our staff and we want to be friendly and kind to them. It sounds like the makings of good friendship except that if we don't pay them to be with us, then they will have to go somewhere else to work. I don't like to think about that, because I don't want my staff to leave us. I think my staff feel bad that they get paid to be with us, sometimes they might be embarrassed. They often tell me that they wish that it wasn't this way. Sometimes we call each other "buddy." I don't want them to ever leave.

One way I deal with this, is that we talk about it a lot. They call me their boss. They answer to me. I sign their time sheets. But I worry about Donna. She no longer understands the difference. She thinks that they are her friends. She is going to be really upset if one of them quits.

Reality is that staff do quit. Sometimes they move away, sometimes they go to school, or change jobs. Usually when a staff quits, we don't see them anymore unless we run into them by accident. It is just a sad fact. It can lead to lots of broken relationships for us. When it happens it is very hurtful. I am lucky that most of my staff have stayed with us for many years.

I did have one staff who quit for another job, but she missed us too much. After my mom died and Laurelle knew that we were going to be alone for Christmas, she invited us to her house. We had Christmas dinner with all of her family and relatives. Ever since then, we go over to her house for every holiday dinner: Easter, Thanksgiving, and Christmas. We always bring a coleslaw so we don't go empty handed.

Chapter 8   People First and Celebrating the End of Institutions

I have been very lucky to be able to represent people with disabilities. When I lived at Rideau I knew that putting thousands of people in an institution was wrong. Watching my friend die is only the most horrible example of why that is true. Every day people were treated badly. Not because all the staff were bad or mean. But because when you put that many people together that the rest of the world does not value, you know that bad things will happen.

[Left to right: Elizabeth Sahl, David Fellows, Joseph Boisvenue, Shane Geraghty, Denise Wright (kneeling), Gord, Donna, Caroline Brown, Reina Soltis]

So when I left there in 1974 I knew that one day I would try to make things better. I'm determined like that.

I connected with People First and other advocacy groups over the years. This chapter tells you how we made things better for other people with disabilities.

People First and the Issues

People First is an international organization representing people who have been labeled with an intellectual disability. I started the People First group in Brockville 30 years ago to help people think about planning their lives. I wanted to help the group get organized.

When I got out of the institution I was looking for a purpose, for something to do. I remember hearing about this guy Peter Park, who started a People First organization. I wanted to do something as well. I wanted to make a difference for other people. I didn't want other people to go through the same thing as me.

[Gord loved going to conferences.
He was always listening intensely.]

People First really woke me up. It made me responsible. I tried to get people to join the movement. I met Peter Park and he told me that I could do this. I have been working hard for People First ever since. People First taught me a lot and grew my confidence. It taught me about my rights. Peter Park and Pat Worth helped me to see how our Brockville group and I could make a real difference.

I went to conferences in Toronto to think about this more. When we got our membership in the provincial and national organizations, we were very excited.

[Gord, Elizabeth Sahl and David Fellows at the Brockville Accessibility Open House]

[Peter Park and Gord became lifelong friends. Peter surprised Gord and Donna by attending their 25th anniversary party.]

There were many issues we looked at over those decades. Here are just a few.

Sterilization of women against their wills. The Eve Case was a big issue when I got involved with People First. It is wrong for women to have their rights taken away from them. It is not fair. People were making decisions about these women's own body and their lives.

Nobody thought about how sterilization would prevent the birth of new babies. Sterilization is a way to prevent the birth of babies with disabilities and tells the rest of us that disabled babies are not good. Some women might want to have a baby and some women wouldn't want to. It doesn't matter. They should just leave women alone. It is wrong to force women to have the operation. I did some reading on it. I talked about it a lot. I went to workshops and asked a whole bunch of questions.

Name Change to Community Living For many years, organizations that were meant to help those of us with a developmental disability were called *Associations for the Mentally Retarded*. People had no idea how hurtful that name was.

Changing the name of all of these local, provincial and the national associations to *Community Living* was a very important thing. Many people thought it was only a symbolic gesture. It was much more than that.

The associations finally listened to the people they were supporting. It may sound like a small thing, but being listened to, is a very powerful feeling. It finally meant that we were part of making decisions for ourselves and about ourselves. Before, both in the institution and in some of the associations, other people were deciding what was best for us.

We were finally being recognized as competent to speak for ourselves. We still needed their support and are grateful that so many people want to help us, but now we felt part of the organizations – we were no longer outsiders.

Now that we had our own associations listening to us and helping us to advocate for ourselves, we could look to the larger community to get them to listen to us as we tried to close down the provincial institutions.

Euthanasia and Assisted Dying People with disabilities are always at risk of losing their rights or even their lives. Euthanasia is another way of saying that someone's life is not worth living. That is always a dangerous belief, especially for people with disabilities.

I was on the council for Community Living Ontario when I first started to learn about it. It was all over the news, and I knew that I had to speak about it. My mom didn't agree with me that euthanasia was wrong. When we first met Denise, a coordinator at BDACI, I decided to test her. I brought up the subject of euthanasia to see what side she was on. Even though she was on my side, she was able to talk to my mom about it without getting her upset. It wasn't a law in Canada yet, but I knew that lots of people wanted it.

I am still hoping the government will keep it illegal. It scares me. It is very dangerous for people with disabilities. People are afraid of disability. They judge us and think that they would rather die than live like we do. We have to keep talking about the danger of euthanasia to help people understand. I

talk about it with both groups that I belonged to — People
First and BDACI.

A time to
remember

EMC photo by STACEY ROY

Gordon Ferguson, president of the Brockville People First, pauses for a moment
of silence with an audience of approximately 60 individuals who attended the
March 31 commemorative event at the BAC, held to mark the end of institutionalization for those with intellectual disabilities in Ontario. Ferguson spoke about
his 16 years at Rideau Regional Centre in Smiths Falls and the unpleasant experiences he had. After watching 'Freedom Tour' the group lit the candle above to
remember those who died in institutions and their hope for the future.

[Gord made the front page of the local weekly newspaper]

Selective Abortions should not happen. Babies are being
killed every day. These are babies with good moms.
Everybody is different and we all have different abilities, but
people are so afraid of disability that they even want to get
rid of the babies! Doctors should not be allowed to abort

babies just because they will have a disability. They are supposed to save people, not kill them.

Selective abortions is another way to tell the world that someone's life is not worth living. Imagine if you saw television news shows, hundreds over the years, telling you that pregnant parents should abort their baby rather than allow them to live the life you have. How would you feel?

You can see why these issues need a lot more talking and a lot more advocacy. Our rights should not be lost and people should not be killed just because other people don't value us. We need to work this out better. We still have a lot of work to do.

Closing the Rideau Regional Centre

On March 31, 2009 we celebrated the closure of the Rideau Regional Centre. I gave a speech at the Brockville Arts Centre and made the newspaper. Fifty-one years after I was admitted to Rideau I helped close it down. What a great feeling it was to watch the institution that hurt so many people close its doors.

Closing institutions is the thing that I am most proud of. This was important because I remembered how the staff treated me. Until 2009 other people were still living there and probably going through some of the same things I did.

It bothered me that other residents didn't know about living in the community… about freedom. Some of them, and their families, were afraid of leaving the institution where they had grown up. However, it was time for a change. We had to get everybody out of there. In 1970 People First told the board at the Community Living conference that we wanted them closed.

Today young people and older people with disabilities are getting put into nursing homes. The government closed institutions only to quietly put some of us into other institutions called nursing homes or long-term care facilities.

This is the new issue that we need to fight. Donna and I almost got institutionalized again. This has to stop.

Thank goodness most of you reading this will probably never have to be involved in such an institutional life nor the fight to close it. I'm proud of how I contributed to closing down this institution but am also sad that we had to fight so hard and so long to get it done. It was wrong from the start. People may have meant well when they started. But it quickly proved to be a place of hurt and pain rather than learning and growth. That it took so long to close down is shameful. I am glad people listened to me and others who shared our stories to help close down Rideau and other provincial institutions.

[Memorial Plaque –"The Honourable Dr. Helena Jaczek, spoke at the commemorative plaque ceremony to honour the memory of former Rideau Regional Centre's residents. The Rideau Regional Plaque Ceremony, December 17, 2014]

[Gord chatting with the Minister of Community and Social Services, Dr. Helena Jaczek, after the ceremony. The ceremony was held at the Smiths Falls Community Memorial Centre. Installing a commemorative plaque is part of the settlement agreement, establishing a $20,619,000 Settlement Fund. The settlement will provide compensation to those people who were residents of the Rideau Regional Centre between 1963 and 2009 and suffered harm.]

In 2015, I received a payment as a member of the class action lawsuit against the province of Ontario for the abuse I suffered while living at Rideau. More importantly, I received an apology. The government apologized for what they had done to me and to thousands of others who lived there. It means a lot to have the Premier tell us they were wrong and we were right.

Community Living Ontario's Role

Community Living Ontario had a Deinstitutionalization Working Group sub-committee that I was on for several years. Our goal was closing all institutions in Ontario for people who have an intellectual disability and, of course, the Rideau Regional Centre was part of that.

We also wanted to make sure that new institutions would never be opened.

We were extremely successful. In 2009 the last three institutions operated by the government were closed including Rideau. The last 1,600 people institutionalized in the province were helped to move into their communities.

It did not go perfectly, of course. Not everyone was happy because they were used to a different life at the institution – a life they could not compare to living in the community. So the change took time for both the people who lived there and their families. I think most would agree that living in the community is better.

Rick Tutt was the chair of this sub-committee at Community Living Ontario. He wrote a note about our success: *"At Community Living Ontario's Annual Meeting in 2009, there was considerable celebration about the closures…it was arguably one of the most important victories in our fifty-year history. Just as the meeting was coming to a close, Gord Ferguson went to the podium and proposed a resolution which has become known as the 'Gord Ferguson Watchdog Resolution' which charges our Association with the responsibility of keeping watch to ensure that we never repeat the terrible history of re-opening or creating new institutions in our province."*

Rick added a note about me that I really appreciate: *"Gord is a dedicated member of this movement and has played an extremely active role in his local and provincial Associations for Community Living and People First (a self advocate's organization) at both the local and provincial level. He is well respected by many people throughout Ontario and indeed throughout Canada."*

Other Advocacy

My mom used to help me with my People First work. At the beginning she helped by driving me to the meetings and was our secretary for a while. When I lost my sight it made it harder but I didn't give up. I kept trying.

My mom supported BDACI but she didn't join as a member – only Donna and I did. She never learned about the issues that are important me. I think the future scared her.

Mom was old school. We lived together for so long that she forgot that we used to live on our own. She liked to think of us as children and often called Donna and me "kids" when she talked about us to other people. This wasn't good because soon everyone else began thinking of us as children and not adults. Mom knew that we needed help and I think she was afraid that we wouldn't listen or make good choices. I think this attitude towards Donna and me affected how the trustees saw us and why they wanted to follow my mom's wishes.

[Sixth Annual Federal Policy Forum. Kory Earle (Past President), Honourable Carla Qualtrough (Federal Minister of Disability and Sport) and Gord Ferguson (Vice President People First of Brockville). Attended the Sixth Annual Federal Policy Forum on Inclusion on December 2nd, 2015. The forum was well attended by many people from all over Canada. The sessions were very informative and provided insight, data and research on disability issues. The forum was hosted by People First of Canada and Canadian Association for Community Living (CACL).]

Why Advocacy is Important to Me

[Gordon speaks when no one else has brought up a point
that he believes needs to be addressed.]

Advocacy is about making a difference – making life better
for other people and for Donna and me. It is important
because the alternative is a place like Rideau where no one
had a voice and bad things, evil things, happened.

Beth French knew how important advocacy is to me. *"He has
been on the BDACI board since the early 90's, and he has been active
on the General Association Committee and been a presence bringing
forward the voice of someone who has lived experiences in
institutionalization and having to fight for his rights as he became a
community member.*

"On one hand there is a contribution that he makes because he brings his insight, his wisdom and his clarity to the board and the committee. He isn't a big talker, so he tends to listen very carefully and then will offer a very succinct and clear comment and often those are right on the money and helpful comments. It conveys a sense that he has been a very quiet, knowledgeable and careful participant.

"On the other hand, he participated in People First Ontario, and Community Living Ontario. He was very proud to be part of, and he brought a sense of activism from Brockville, which was important for the others to learn about, and also important for Brockville's image and the impression that others would have of us. At the provincial level in the self-advocacy movement and the association, he did a great deal by being willing to participate when very few others have been willing. He conveyed a sense that Brockville cares about what is happening provincially and is willing to contribute. He took one for the team. That was a great benefit to BDACI.

"I know that he is proud of that participation, but he certainly made a bona fide contribution for doing that. It was more than something that was interesting for Gord -- it was very helpful and important to BDACI."

[Advocacy work or not, the dishes still need to get done.]

I won the Brockville & District Association Community Involvement's Community Involvement award in 2000. I also won BDACI's President's Award in 2010. In 2015, People First of Brockville won the James Montgomery Community Award for the work that we did in organizing the Community Forum, the Mayor's Debate, and the Federal Candidates Meet-and-Greet. I was the chair of the committee that organized these things.

[President Bobbi Stephens presents Gord
with the 2010 President's Award.]

I don't do things to earn awards; I do it because it is important and right. But winning an award is nice because it is a way for me to know that my work means something to other people. It is a formal thank you and that means a lot to me. You can imagine that in my years at Rideau, I did not get thanked a lot for my ideas and my work. That stays with you for many years afterward. So these awards tell me that people think I was right to fight to get out of Rideau, to close it down, and to help others.

[Gord gave the welcome speech at the Federal Candidates 'Meet and Greet.']

With these public forums, bringing in politicians and getting them to focus on issues that affect people with disabilities, helps everyone realize that our issues are important. For the first time we are seen as people who are voters, decision makers. We are important. They need our votes. We are involved in our community. We had the newspapers there, and lots of people showed up to listen to the politicians. It helped other people with disabilities understand their right to vote and to decide who to vote for. I got to meet all the candidates.

I love to give speeches. Even today I like doing it because I still have a lot to say and I like to show people that I can do more than they thought. Sure I get nervous before I give a speech, but I want to show people what I can do. It is good for all people with disabilities. One of my big problems today is that I can no longer see enough to read. So my supporters and I figured out a way to use technology to help me. My worker reads the speech into his iPhone, then we use Face Time to connect wirelessly with my iPad which is connected to my earpiece and I repeat it into the microphone. It works great.

[Gord giving a speech with Joseph Boisvenue holding the microphone.]

By giving speeches and using technology like this, we are showing other people that they can do more than they thought. They just need to be creative and not give up. I like it when people say to me "Good idea! I am going to try that too."

Chapter 9   Our New Home Life

My Home

I am the boss of my own home now. My staff have to knock on the door and I let them in when they arrive for their shift. They ask permission before they go into my bedroom or go through my stuff. I decide what we eat for supper. Donna or I answer the phone when it rings. Donna and I live here, my staff doesn't. It's our home.

Back when we first got married, we were supported by staff from another agency who thought that they could come into my home and boss us around. They told me what we could and couldn't do, what I could spend my money on and what I couldn't. They wanted me to do things their way. It felt like they were trying to take over our lives. It made me feel angry and I stopped listening to them. I eventually had enough, and nicely showed them the door.

I was protecting my home. I needed workers to help us, but they shouldn't come in and tell me what to do or make me feel bad. How do they help us without taking over with us? By listening more than talking. By asking more than telling. By offering help more than taking over.

So we were left with no one to help us. After a while my Mom asked us to live with her. Living together benefited each of us. It wasn't just Mom trying to be nice. We helped her as much as she helped us.

Through my adult life I needed a home and I also needed support. Those are two different things. I now get the kind of support I have always needed – an understanding of what it means to separate home from support.

They need to be and stay separate. For example, if my staff now are mad at me for some reason, they can't kick me out. My home is mine. I don't have to move out unless I want to move. Nobody can take it away from me. I am safe here. The workers are providing support so that I can live in my home and do the things that I want to do. That is all.

I am proud of my home. I love living here with Donna. Home is someplace safe, someplace where I can be myself. I can relax here when I am with Donna. It is someplace where I can sleep well. Home is a feeling, where I can be myself. It is where my heart is. Home is where I can make my own rules, and I can do what I want to do.

I can make an apartment or house a home, but not an institution or nursing home.

I try to teach everybody about what a home is. Home is a place where you can make your own decisions. You can go outside if you want to or not. It is also a place to put my stuff and keep my collections.

Supporters that Help

Staff shouldn't feel that they know better. Staff have to respect the people and their ways. One of my supporters, Denise, has become a strong advocate for me. She is helping me write this book, for example. We sit and talk. She asks questions and I give her answers that she writes down. Later she types them up for me. If not for her, you would not be reading this book.

But she does not write the book for me. She does not tell me what to say and what not to say. This is my book and she helps me pull together all of my thoughts. That is the difference between a supporter now and 30 years ago.

Thirty years, no supporter would have helped me write a book. They would have told me that no one would be interested. No one was interested in our lives at Rideau 40 years ago. Even if someone had shown interest, they would have told me what to write. They would have taken over.

My support workers help me get outside, go shopping, go to meetings and do the things that are important. One of my support workers, Shane Geraghty takes me to the meetings, helps me get ready for the meetings — like reading to me all the paperwork and the last board minutes so I know what we will be talking about. We talk about the issues, so that I will be ready. When I have to do a speech he helps me practice. Now that I can't see enough to read due to my eye problems, he figures out a way to help me. I gave a speech at the Mayor's Debate, the Community Forum and also the All Candidates Meeting with his help.

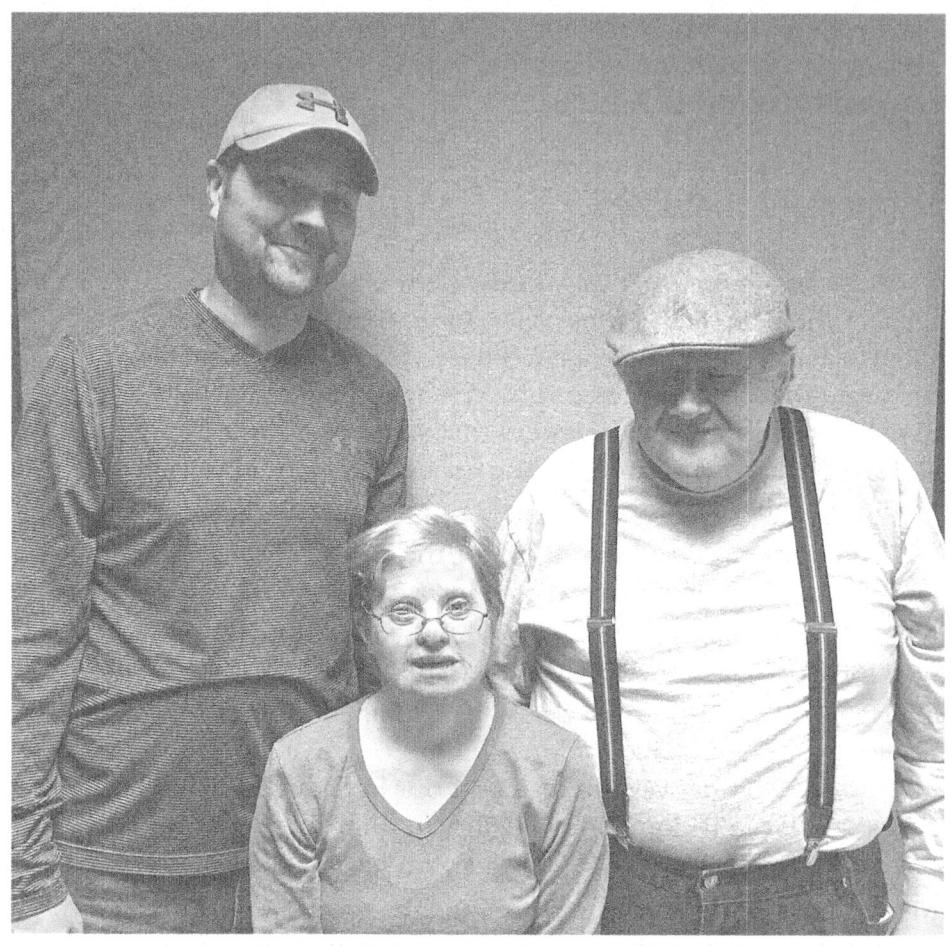

[Shane, Donna and Gord]

Shane's wife cuts my hair. I like going to her because I trust her. They know me. I get special treatment when I go there. They make sure my chair is waiting for me. I get treated like a king there.

I have known Shane for four years. Shane saved my life twice when I was choking. He feels like my buddy now. I trust him. He has my back.

Shane helps me translate information into plain language. He teaches me and sometimes I teach him. We have good discussions about the topics that are important to me, like sports, euthanasia and politics. There is more to support than just making sure I am clean, showered, and in the right place at the right time.

Shane writes: "I know Gord very well. Before a meeting or speech I do a play-by-play with him. At the meeting, I quietly inform him who is around, where and how many tables there are, that the canteen is to the left, who is sitting at our table, etc. I am his eyes. We always rehearse like crazy before, not only his speech but also what it is going to be like, how many people, who is going to be there, and what is the purpose of the meeting or speech.

"I want to make sure that he is fully prepared. I have high expectations of what Gord is capable of doing. Gord has to fulfill a role, and he relies on me to do his job. How people see Gord in public is very important. I have a lot of respect for him, so I want to ensure that everyone sees the exact same human being that I see every day.

"He is someone who has a lot of courage and teaches everyone a lot about life. Gord has taught and changed me a lot. The first thing I learned was the difference between a home and a place where someone lives. When you live in a group home or an institution you don't own anything You just exist in a place. Home is where you find your identity and your confidence.

"After Gord's mom passed away, Gord changed. He talked about his house every day. His confidence grew. He made me realize how important it was to have a place that you call home. To feel like you belong. When Gord started living in his own home, he changed.

"My first three shifts were sitting in Gord's house with his mom going through photo albums talking all about Gord. I wasn't allowed to leave. Gord didn't say a thing. She wouldn't let me talk. When I first started Gord was definitely in the son role. He did as he was told, and didn't argue. He only spoke when he was spoken to. It was very quiet in the house. Mom ruled the nest.

"When I used to come, Gord would sit in his chair, and everything was brought to him. He didn't have control over anything at home, but he was served well. Mom was a good cook and she would make lots of desserts. Gord was well looked after, but he had no choice about anything. His outside work in advocacy gave him that sense of control. At home Gord would not talk about himself, only about mom. He could not dream or talk about his future, only about the good old days.

"After his mom passed away, Gord found his voice. He changed from a boy to a man. He then started talking about his responsibilities to pay the bills. He wanted to take charge of his home and make it his own. Gord wanted to change things. Over the process Gord grew into the homeowner role: talking about arranging cutting the lawn, paying his mortgage and taxes. He had responsibilities. It changed his whole outlook on life itself. How he treated his workers. He used to be submissive with his workers, and now he acts like their boss. Now he says no to me or tells me to stop arguing with him. Owning the house really changed Gord.

"I have had the privilege of taking Gord and Donna to several sporting events. It is amazing to see them having fun. Their support needs are secondary to the fact that they are included and part of a bigger event. We are part the atmosphere, and we get caught up in the action. I use a lot of humour.

"We are open and approachable to people. Once, we went to Toronto to a Blue Jays game and we rode the train. We had so much fun... we were the party. We had people eight rows around us laughing with us. We met other baseball fans on the way to the game, and talked to us the whole way up. It made the train ride go really fast, and they even walked with us up to the stadium. By the time we got to Toronto, we were excited and ready for the game.

"I know that Gord can't see what is happening so I use my words to explain the situation to everyone including Gord. I am like the interpreter. I always make sure that I include

Gord in the conversation. I talk to other people around, to engage them with Gord. I talk about Gord's love for baseball and the Blue Jays, to give them something in common. Finding common ground is important for everyone to join the conversation; I keep including Gord, and talking about what he loves.

"I always make sure that we are talking about a topic that Gord likes and that he would have something to contribute. I basically brag about him, and he would get excited and join in. 'Oh Gord, remember when you told me this....' or I make a joke about him dozing. 'Oh he is just tired. Come on old man get up' and Gord would automatically jump up and smile. Everyone including Gord would start laughing, which brings humour to an awkward situation.

"This way people wouldn't be looking at him and wondering what was wrong with him. Somebody once called me his grandson, and I thought that it was better not to correct the person. We didn't push it but we didn't deny it either. We want to make sure that the imagery is as positive as possible, and for this person the grandpa and grandson relationship was more positive than disabled person and worker relationship. So we went with it for that time only, we just didn't correct him. It was our private joke."

I used to be very quiet. I didn't like speaking my mind because I was scared that someone was going to hurt me. I can't see them coming anymore, so I can't fight back. That's a good thing about Maggie our dog; she warns me when people are here.

There is a difference between supporting and teaching someone. Staff are supposed to help us to do the things we can't do. They are supposed to help us and not make us feel bad that we can't do something or when we make mistakes. They are supposed to help not be hurtful.

Individualized Funding

All the support in the world is not possible without funding. There are resources to pay for health care and basic personal care (1 hour a day) but that is not enough. We need support to live the life that other people may take for granted. That can only happen through individualized funding.

Individualized funding is very important to me. Without it I would not be able to live in my home. Right now we don't have enough guaranteed funding to meet all of our needs, even though it would cost a lot more for us to live in a group home or a nursing home and we would get a lot less support. We don't have enough funding to pay for the support that Donna and I need, but the service providers in Brockville understand how important it is to us. Somehow they have always managed to find enough "emergency funding" each year so that we can have the support that we need.

I want to thank them for this. I am glad that we live in Brockville where people understand and care. Every few months, BDACI has to go to these meetings to ask for more money. I would worry a lot less if we didn't have to keep asking for the money. It would be nice if I could just worry about what I wanted to do each day instead.

Individualized funding lets Donna and me live together as a married couple in our own home the way we want to live. We don't have to move out into another place like a group home or a nursing home. Individualized funding lets us use the money the way that works for us. Soon, we will be getting a tenant downstairs in our home to make things a little cheaper. We are constantly trying to find ways to make things cheaper and easier for everyone.

Supporting a Marriage to Stay Strong

In 2008 the doctor's diagnosed Donna with Alzheimer's or "old-timers" as she used to say.

[Gord and Donna and their little dog, Maggie.]

Even though she is doing a good job fighting it, I can see the changes in her. Also, both of her parents died from cancer many years ago, and my mom died of cancer in 2011. When she heard that I had cancer early in 2015, she was pretty upset. She did a good job looking after me when I was sick with chemo, but I could tell from the way that she acted that she was worried and stressed.

I was pretty worried about her as she got more and more stressed and she started getting angry and frustrated. It wasn't like her to have meltdowns, and to yell at our staff. I had to figure something out fast. We had lots of meetings with my staff and supporters to try to figure out some answers.

We had a doctor tell us that we needed to put her on a behaviour program. That didn't make sense to me. First we had to find a way to help Donna sleep better. And then we had to focus on the good qualities of our marriage. Donna is a very touchy-feely kind of woman. She loves to cuddle and hug. That was my job. When she started to get upset, I would sit beside her on the couch and offer to talk to her and hug her. After a few minutes, she and I would start talking about something else and she forgot what she was upset about. Soon we were both laughing and having a good time. I am the only one who can help Donna. She needs me!

Beth French got it: *"I think their marriage played a significant role in terms of building relationships for Gord and Donna. People respected their commitment to each other, and their marriage. When they*

married, it was a relatively new thing to occur, so they were seen as trail blazers, and the fact that their marriage has lasted for so long is a testament to their love and commitment. When they celebrated their 25th anniversary they included so many people in it. It was a factor in bringing people into their circle because many people can relate to their love. In fact the team of people who helped them out, were people who had committed relationships themselves, and felt somewhat allied with Gord and Donna, and it gave them a common understanding."

Epilogue

My cousin Marilyn Gibson, saw a sign recently that said, *"When you can tell your story without crying, you have healed."*

I think that in retelling my stories for you, I have been partially healed. Most of the stories do not cause the pain they once did. Getting older helps with that.

My Aunt Jean says that this book is a healing project for me. She understands that part of this book's goal is to bring our extended family back together. My mom's Trustees and I have had some differences but not because we did not like each other – but because we did and we wanted the best for each other. We just disagreed, for a while, about what that 'best' was and how to achieve it – and now we agree.

I hope that my stories help you in some way. Help you to look deeper into the lives of the people around you. We are all hurt. We have all felt grief, pain and a deep sense of being alone in this world.

My stories might help you with your stories. My life might help you help others with their lives.

But in the end, we all have to live our own lives as best we can. If my stories help you fulfill some of your dreams, that is wonderful. If my stories help you with your own long-term relationships, that is great. And if my stories mean that when we meet we might become friends or even better friends, then it was all worth the effort.

I have cancer so I may not live as long a life as I wanted. I hope that these stories will mean that I will live longer through you. I hope that you will take my stories to help hundreds, if not thousands of people live a better life. If you do that then my years of at Rideau and the struggles of getting the life that I love will have purpose. And maybe, my friend Caesar, who died at Rideau, and all of the other people who suffered and died there for no reason, will also be remembered.

It will all have been worth it then. This is what I want my legacy to be.

Afterword
(by Denise Wright)

Gord has many amazing qualities, but the one that I admire the most is his ability to see the positive in each situation. He never feels sorry for himself and he never acts like a victim. Even today, he would rather talk about the good memories that he had of Rideau then talk about the bad ones. He is also quick to point out that many good staff worked there too.

[Denise Wright and Gord]

After he left Rideau, he started to live life on his terms. Imagine how hard it must have been to get a job, pass his driver's license, buy a car, and then convince the world that you should be allowed to get married to the one that you love. He didn't give up. He doesn't give up. He just keeps going.

When I met him, one of the first things that he told me was not to rush him. He needed more time than others to think about things before he could make a comment. Gord knew what he needed. He wasn't embarrassed and he didn't feel the need to apologize. He was just being clear. It is up to us to give him time and space, and when he is given the supports and accommodations that he needs he will be able to participate at his very best with deep insight.

Gord is a quiet and humble leader. He knows what he wants to do and quietly finds a way to do it. He leads by example. He shows people what is important to him in a situation, and he just goes out and does it. He enjoys the spotlight, but he doesn't seek it out. Life hasn't been easy for Gord, and he doesn't hold grudges. He is an eternal optimist. His hope for the future and positive outlook on life has been the determining factor to his success. He is loyal and committed to the values that he holds dear to his heart. He knows what is right and what he needs in his life, and he is not afraid to stand up and talk about it.

There are very few people who are worthy of being called a hero, and Gord is one of them. He makes me want to be a better person.

Student/Book Club Questions

Gord has attended Dr. Wolf Wolfensberger's *Social Role Valorization* workshops as well as two weekend conferences called *A Good Life*. Dr. Wolfensberger greatly affected Gord's thoughts and as a result how he lived his life. As you read this book, perhaps you can reflect on the following themes from Dr. Wolfensberger's work:

The Good Things in Life

1. What good things in life does Gord enjoy?
2. What factors led to Gord having the good things in life?
3. In what ways are Gord and Donna vulnerable? What safeguards need to be in place to address these vulnerabilities?
4. Gord's story is compelling. Some might think this kind of story could not happen anywhere else. Do you think it would be possible to assist other people to have such rewarding lives? What would it take to do that?
5. What personal qualities and skills does Gord possess that have led to him being so successful?

Wounds

1. Please provide an analysis of the wounds that Gord experienced.
2. How did these wounds increase his vulnerability?

Roles

1. What valued roles has Gord had in his life? How did these roles affect him?

2. What devalued roles did he hold when he was younger? How did those roles affect him? What devalued roles does he hold now?

3. Gord and Donna started out their marriage living in their own apartment before they moved in with his mom. For a while the three of them were all homeowners, but eventually Gord and Donna gave up that role. After many years of living with his mother, Gord and Donna were perceived as being incapable of living on their own. How did losing these positive roles increase their vulnerabilities?

4. Which is more powerful: the negative roles or the positive ones? Why?

5. As Gord's disabilities increased (loss of his eyesight, aging), he became more vulnerable to the devalued roles. What could be done to compensate against this?

Friends

1. What roles did friends play in Gord's life? Are there somethings that only friends (not staff) could do?

2. One of the remarkable things about this story is the fact that Gord has had many long term friends. This is very unusual for many people with disabilities. Why do you think that this is case? How might you try to foster these kinds of long term relationships for people you know and support?

3. Many people in Gord's life went "above and beyond" to make sure they could assist Gord and Donna. In what ways did they extend themselves? What risk or sacrifices might others have made? Why? What personal qualities did the people who helped Gord and Donna possess? What values do you think that they held?

Paid Support

1. Describe how staff have helped Gord to have a better image?

2. How has the staff helped to connect him in a positive way to others?

3. Develop some guidelines to help the paid staff support Gord and Donna in a positive way? Include the different roles of direct staff and administrators.

4. Gord acknowledges the complexities of his staff developing close personal relationships with him and Donna. Often staff introduce them to their family and friends. He knows from experience that once his staff quit and move on with their lives, that they will not likely see him again. The issue becomes magnified when the staff's family doesn't maintain the relationship either. How big of an issue is this really? What safeguards can be put in place to help mitigate this?

5. What are the dangers of his staff calling him "a friend"?

6. Staff did many things to help Gord and Donna that were "not in the job description". What were those things? Why do you think that they did that? Could you see yourself emulating their model?

SRV Themes

1. Consider each of the 10 themes for SRV and connect each theme to situations in Gord's life. Comment on how each theme was or could be employed to craft and maintain valued roles.

2. How could the SRV themes be used to continue to support Gord and Donna to have a good life?

INDEX

Made in the USA
Monee, IL
10 June 2026

52191939R00075